THE LOCH NESS MONSTER
THE EVIDENCE

A critical evaluation of the principal
evidence for the existence of the
most famous lake-monster in the world.

By the same author

The UFO Mystery Solved
The Rise and Fall of Jesus

Steuart Campbell is a science writer and broadcaster
and author of many articles and books on mysteries.
He has a degree in science and mathematics.

THE LOCH NESS MONSTER
THE EVIDENCE

Steuart Campbell

Birlinn

This revised edition published in 2002 by
Birlinn Limited
West Newington House
10 Newington Road
Edinburgh
EH3 9DQ

www.birlinn.co.uk

First published in 1986 by
The Aquarian Press
Revised and reprinted in 1991 by
Aberdeen University Press
First published by Birlinn Ltd in 1996

ISBN 1 84158 198 4

British Library Cataloguing-in-Publication Data
A catalogue record for this book is available
from the British Library

Typeset by Brinnoven, Livingston
Printed and bound by Antony Rowe Ltd, Chippenham

Contents

List of Illustrations

List of Tables

Acknowledgements

I acknowledge the assistance of the following individuals: Peter F. Baker, Henry H. Bauer, Janet Bord, Alastair and Sue Boyd, Jim Buchanan, Maurice Burton, Miles Cato, David Creasey, Harold E. Edgerton, R. B. Davenport, Hilary Green, Alan Gillespie, Rip Hepple, Tony Harmsworth, Ricky Gardiner, Waldemar Lehn, Gordon Mackintosh, Dick Raynor, Robert H. Rines, Chris Rutkowski, Tony Shiels, Adrian Shine, Alan Wilkins, Nicolas Witchell; and the following organisations: BUE Subsea Ltd, East Kent Maritime Trust, Forestry Commission, Honeywell Inc. (Marine Systems Division), Institute of Oceanographic Sciences, Johnsons of Hendon, Kelvin Hughes, Kodak Ltd, Marconi International Marine, Oceano Instruments (UK) Ltd, Raytheon Marine Sales and Service Co. Also the following libraries: British Library Document Supply Centre, Edinburgh Central Library, Edinburgh University Library, Inverness Central Library, Library of the Royal Museum of Scotland (Chambers St.), National Library of Scotland.

Note on Terminology

To save space, and to avoid the problem of whether or not to refer to a 'monster', the very existence of which is here in question, I shall refer to the Loch Ness monster as N. This stands for 'Nessie', or the creatures it represents, either singly or as a group, as described by believers and witnesses and in conformity with the myth that has developed around the concept. The use of the term does not imply my acceptance of the existence of any particular unknown creature in Loch Ness. The names of other lake-monsters will be abbreviated similarly.

Loch is Gaelic for the English 'lake', although it is also used for firths, or sea inlets. However, in English, the habit has become established of describing Scottish lakes as 'lochs' (likewise every Scottish mountain is 'ben' and every valley is 'glen'). This is sheer linguistic snobbery, exhibited by people pretending to know Gaelic. Since I write in English I shall use the English word for 'a large body of water entirely surrounded by land'. Nevertheless place-names will be respected (including 'Loch' where quoted), but 'Loch', 'Lough' and 'Lake' will be abbreviated to L where possible. This may help to avoid what I once saw at the hand of an American writer – 'Lake Loch Ness'!

Some of the data presented here is techical and quantitative. Because mensuration is SI (*Système International*) metric, readers who are not familiar with the system may wish to be reminded of the following abbreviations. The principal units (in this book) are the unit of length, the metre (m); the unit of mass, the kilogram (kg); the unit of time, the second (s); the unit of power, the watt (W); and the unit of frequency, the hertz (Hz). For temperatures I shall use the non-SI unit, the degree Celsius (°C), and other non-SI units will be the unit of plane angle, the degree (. . °); the unit of time, the minute (min); the unit of mass, 1000 kg (tonne); and the unit of speed, the kilometre per hour (km/h). The energy of strobe lights is expressed in the watt-second (Ws), a non-SI unit which actually equals the joule (J). Subdivisions and multiples of the principal units are indicated by prefixes, as follows:

one thousandth	= milli- (m)
one hundredth	= centi- (c)
one thousand times	= kilo- (k)
one million times	= mega- (M)

Mass is not the same as weight, but for most practical purposes may be taken to be so. Non-metric units in quotations have been given approximate metric equivalents which may appear to imply precision that was not originally implied. Similarly some metric quantities will appear to be precise only because they are a conversion from a rounded non-metric quantity.

Use will be made of some abbreviations, as follows: MIT = Massachusetts Institute of Technology; JPL = Jet Propulsion Laboratory (Caltech): BBC = British Broadcasting Corporation; ITN = Independent Television News; JARIC = Joint Air Reconnaissance Intelligence Centre; and CRO = cathode-ray oscilloscope.

1

Prologue:
A Preparation and Background

The Origin of Belief in N

The existence of N was announced in 1933, apparently after a spectacular demonstration (though see p. 18), but the announcement owed much to the personal beliefs of a local water bailiff, Alex Campbell. Among other things (he distorted the account in a number of ways) he alleged that what had been seen was the 'water kelpie', a 'fearsome-looking monster' that had 'for generations' been credited with living in L Ness.[1] Many readers of his report must have wondered why, if N had lived for so long in the lake, they had not heard of it before. In fact there had been previous reports, but for various reasons these had not been relayed by newspapers outside Scotland. Others have dealt with the reason for N's sudden notoriety and here we are more concerned with the evidence for its existence. However, it is relevant to ask about the tradition to which Alex Campbell referred.

There was a widespread Highland belief that a water horse or kelpie inhabited not only L Ness but nearly every lake in Scotland. It was said to be an evil spirit which not only lured travellers to their death by drowning but took a delight in doing so. Because this explained why people drowned in lakes it may be concluded that the myth originated from a *need* to explain such drownings. Moon records that when a swimming horse disappeared in the middle of L Okanagan (see p. 90) the drowning was attributed to the presence of the lake demon, later identified with the monster Ogopogo.[2] Often the body never reappeared and it must have been assumed that it had been taken to some other world. This is certainly true of L Ness, which is wrongly thought never to give up its dead.

In Ireland, where the Scots originated, the country people supposed that this world is duplicated underwater, and they told tales of cows, bulls, dogs, and horses from that other-world. Sometimes these animals were captured, the water horses being broken to the plough.[3] In certain legends the water animals had other-world owners, suggesting a belief in a mirror other-world in lakes and pools. According to this conception man possesses the land, while water becomes the special preserve of the other-world.[4] This idea of an inverted world may have come from sight of the reflection of the 'upper' world in calm water surfaces. A reflection was a mysterious phenomenon to primitive peoples, who usually gave it mystical qualities.

If water was the domain of the other-world, then those who ventured onto lakes were violating that world and were in danger of punishment. Necessarily folklore must have developed around this concept, and any unusual lake phenomenon must have been interpreted as a manifestation of this underworld. Because there was a general belief in the existence of the underworld and its creatures it was inevitable that some would claim to have seen these creatures (there are always those who claim to have seen what others have merely postulated). These reports must then have fed and reinforced the myth. However, as Grimshaw and Lester have warned, it is a mistake to place reliance on the myth as evidence for N's existence: 'the presence/non-presence of an item in the framework of the myth is simply incommensurate with the question of existence/non-existence'.[5] In effect, the myth can be explained without the existence of N, and it offers no kind of substantial evidence for N. Mackal notes that the belief of the Potawatomi tribe, that monsters live in both L Maniton (Devil's L) near Rochester in northern Indiana, and Bass L, seems to be derived from the widespread remains of (fossilised) mastodon bones throughout the area. The Indians concluded that the bones are those of lake monsters whose descendants still inhabit the lakes, and this belief was later transmitted to the settlers, who also feared the lakes.[6]

Grimshaw and Lester noted that the sinister kelpie contrasts remarkably with the harmless lovable modern N. They attributed this conversion to the interest in prehistoric monsters stimulated by the concrete models shown at the Great Exhibition in the Crystal Palace (London) in 1851.[7] Monsters of all sorts then entered the popular imagination and a belief in sea serpents developed. As early as 1859 Philip Gosse popularised the plesiosaur as an explanation for the mystery of the sea serpent. Folklore thus modernised itself by adapting to the findings of science.[8] When Gould explained N as a lake-locked sea serpent it was inevitable that the former would then be regarded as a plesiosaur. This notion has been particularly persistent, despite the lack of evidence for sea serpents, or the implausibility of Gould's hypothesis (that a sea serpent had somehow travelled unseen up the River Ness).

We see therefore that there is no reliable ancient tradition for N, whose origin lies in superstition and confused zoology. Tradition itself offers no evidence for N, and there is no reason to associate modern reports with the tradition. The association made by Alex Campbell was completely unjustified and betrayed his ignorance of the origin of the myth. If N exists then that existence can only be determined by modern evidence. It is as if we wipe out all previous ideas and ask *de novo* whether or not an unknown aquatic species inhabits L Ness (and other lakes). Unconcerned about the reasons why anyone should believe in the existence of N, we may examine the modern evidence in a detached manner.

On Evidence

Evidence is a term that requires definition. Evidence is testimony or facts in support of or for a conclusion, and in science it usually means data in support of a hypothesis. Here the hypothesis is that an unknown aquatic species (N) lives in L Ness; this may be called H_n. Hypotheses usually exist to explain some phenomenon, and evidently H_n exists to explain many alleged anomalous phenomena reported from L Ness. On the other hand, it maybe that all the phenomena have simple explanations, and that it is only because of the existence of H_n (whose origin we have already explored) that the phenomena are thought to be anomalous. In that case N does not exist and the null hypothesis (H_o) is appropriate.

Costello believes that there is sufficient evidence for the existence of N to satisfy a 'scrupulous historian'. I doubt that, but in any case it is not a matter for historians. There must be sufficient evidence to satisfy a physical scientist, preferably a zoologist, although he would not be the best person to examine the available evidence, much of which involves complex technology and physics. But what constitutes evidence? As Bauer has noted, it is by no means obvious what is evidence and what is not; what is thought to be evidence by one person will be thought irrelevant by another. Further, much of the evidence is circumstantial and it is not easy to get access to the original evidence.[9] It seems sensible to take as the primary evidence that which is presented by the majority of the monster-hunters (necessarily believers in the existence of N). However, for the sake of completeness I shall at least list all known instrumental evidence, some of which has already been repudiated by the principal hunters. Discarded evidence will be given less space than that which the hunters themselves regard as important. The onus of proof is always on those who claim to have discovered an anomaly, and in this case it rests on those who claim to have evidence for the existence of N. Despite the fact that they have not thoroughly proved their case, the evidence they present deserves to be examined.

Something needs to be said about negative evidence. Modern science regards a hypothesis as scientific (i.e. in the true spirit of science) if it produces testable predictions. If the tests produce a positive result then that does not prove that the hypothesis is correct, although it might be; it only shows that it has not been found to be incorrect. If the tests produce a negative result, that does not mean that the hypothesis was false, although it might be. Falsification only means that the hypothesis has been contradicted in given conditions. Nevertheless evidence inconsistent with a hypothesis is usually taken as falsification. Here we have two, and only two, rival hypotheses, H_n and H_o. Each makes a prediction, the one that L Ness holds N, and the other that it does not hold N. Both hypotheses are testable (and so, scientific). In fact they are testable by the same experiment, namely a thorough search of L Ness. Short of such a conclusive test, there is bound to be what is considered to be incidental positive and negative evidence We shall examine the claims for positive evidence, but the negative evidence tends to be overlooked. Thousands of people each year look at L Ness and do not see N; hundreds take pictures which do not show N. Here we can only deal with the negative evidence produced by the failure of purposeful searches, but when considering the positive evidence (much of which will turn out to be negative) readers should remember its relationship to a mass of unrecorded negative evidence.

Strictly speaking evidence is not really evidence until it has passed a number of stringent tests. Thus in a court, while a witness may give his evidence, what he says may only be regarded as relevant evidence if it withstands cross-examination. Similarly in science, prima facie evidence must be examined critically, and only if it withstands that examination can it be regarded as sound evidence. The evidence for N stands as prima facie evidence until it has been examined, and it remains to be seen whether or not, after examination, there is any good evidence for the existence of N.

The Evidence for N

What evidence are we looking for? If N exists then it ought to be seen at the surface, at least occasionally. Sometimes it ought to be seen close enough for witnesses to give a good description, and all the descriptions should be consistent. People who live around the lake, or who travel on it regularly, ought to see it frequently. If N is amphibious then we would expect the occasional report of it on the shore, leaving detectable tracks, or even footprints. Since many people, particularly tourists, carry cameras (still and cine) we should expect there to be good photographic evidence.

We should expect N-hunters to be particularly successful at obtaining evidence. Having gone equipped to obtain evidence there should be no difficulty in taking good photographs or making other reliable instrumental records. Indeed, if N exists then it should be possible to capture a live specimen for examination. In addition there should be ample evidence of continued habitation in L Ness; the remains of dead N should be lying on the floor of the lake. Due to poor visibility little success would be expected from underwater photography. However, N ought to be detectable with sonar. In fact, since N itself could not see underwater, it must be expected that it would use echo location to find its prey (presumably fish) and to communicate. The sounds produced by N in these processes ought to be detectable very easily.

Dispelling Some Myths

Although there is no space to explain the geography and biology of L Ness, some facts must be explained.

Many believe that N entered L Ness through an underwater tunnel, and there is a persistent belief in underwater caves, which N might inhabit. Since L Ness is 16 m above sea level, any tunnel large enough to take N would drain the lake down to sea level. There is no tunnel. Nor are there underwater caves; L Ness lies in a glaciated valley ground smooth by aeons of glaciers. Some believe that N entered L Ness from the open sea, and that the lake was a firth for a time after the last ice-age. Although the melting ice raised the sea level, the removal of the ice burden allowed the land also to rise. It has not yet been established that L Ness was ever open to the sea, and the likelihood is that it was not.

Sources of Deception at L Ness

In order to evaluate the evidence for N it is necessary to be able to distinguish it from phenomena which, while they have nothing to do with it, may not be recognised for what they are by the inexperienced. We may call these phenomena 'sources of deception', in that they tend to deceive the inexperienced into thinking that they are manifestations of N. Here I survey those sources of deception above water; those below water relate specifically to sonar, and are dealt with in chapter 6. Above-water sources of deception may be classified as atmospheric, water surface, inanimate objects and animals.

Atmospheric sources of deception. Although there is one report of a surveyor momentarily thinking that some cloud shadows were N,[10] the principal atmospheric phenomenon is the mirage. There is a tradition that on a calm morning in winter and spring observers near water level can see distorted promontories and ships appearing to float in the air.[11] This phenomenon was attributed to cold air lying over warmer water, although this produces an inferior mirage (which may account for the observation if the sky was seen below the direct images). In summer, conditions might arise for the production of a superior mirage where objects over the horizon can become visible on or above the horizon.

Sources of deception in the water surface. Apart from mirages, calm weather brings a water surface that is susceptible to a number of phenomena (it also brings good visibility and an increase in the number of observers). A large lake is capable of very many surface effects, not all of which are familiar to the average observer. Some are natural and some are man-made. Among the former are those caused by wind (e.g. windrows, which appear as dark patches on a brighter background) and those caused by earth tremors (e.g. seiches). But the most important surface source of deception is one made by man.

Although, in rough weather, boat wakes are very soon broken up and dispersed by the waves, in calm conditions they persist and are very prominent. A wake consists of a series of individual wavefronts which move at an angle to the line of the wake. Consequently, from a low angle, the wake can appear as a series of humps travelling across the surface. Such an explanation has been postulated for Ogopogo the phenomenon of L Okanagan in Canada.[12] In calm conditions a wake may travel a great distance. In fact there is a type of wave called a soliton which travels great distances without losing much energy; it was first noticed on a canal when a barge stopped suddenly. Complications set in when two wakes intersect; even though the individual wakes may not have been very obvious, when they cross constructive interference can cause an obvious hump of water that will move in a direction different from that of either wake, appearing to make its own wake. Baker and Westwood noticed that such a hump, after appearing to remain stationary for some time, would suddenly leap forward across the water, giving the impression of a bow wave and following wake. They noticed that very impressive 'monsters' with one or more humps were formed, and that the effect occurred up to half an hour after a boat had passed. In spite of regular traffic through the lake, it was rare enough to take even the most experienced observers by surprise. They concluded that it was most likely that all the multi-humped N were really such wake effects.[13] British Waterways' Chief Engineer in Scotland (R. B. Davenport) has seen N-like wave interference effects on L Ness. He noted that an 'eruption of humps' occurred when the outgoing wake of a craft intersected the return wake when such a craft turned. It could also occur when the wakes of two different craft, travelling in opposite directions, meet.[14] A vessel's stern wave also causes a 'trail of obedient humps which seem to be towed by the vessel'.[15]

Where the shore of L Ness is steep, an incoming wake will be reflected back out again, perhaps modulating an incoming wake 'carving it up in a smooth and regular manner';[15] Mackal described how the two reflections from each shore converge a long way behind a boat to form 'what looks for all the world like the disturbance caused by a partially submerged creature swimming in a straight line'. He also noted that a similar effect was produced close inshore when the shore-reflected bow waves intersects with the incoming stern wave from a large boat.[16] Burton also noticed these 'standing waves' (they are really interference effects, see Plate I). They may be stationary or moving, and they may not appear until the vessel which caused them is out of sight. On one occasion he saw a steamer's wash, when it reached the opposite shore, produce an animal-like brown and glistening hump with foam at one end like a lashing tail.[17]

When a water wave reaches shallow water it breaks when the bottom of the energy system is forced up by the shelving bottom. A large vessel can cause a deep wave disturbance that may not be visible until it is forced to break in shallows. Then a sudden upheaval may occur. Conditions for such upheavals exist at either end of L Ness and in Urquhart Bay.

One of the major causes of N-like wakes on L Ness was British Waterways' converted ice-breaker tug *Scot II*, which operated on the

Plate I: A standing wave captured on video by an anonymous tourist at L Ness on 21 July 1992. The wave rolls over and over but does not move.

Caledonian Canal from 1931. From 1960 to 1991 it carried tourists on cruises according to a strict timetable (see Table 1).[18] It is no longer on the Canal.

Table 1:
Timetable for *Scot II*'s summer cruises on L Ness (times in BST)

	Late April to end of September	Early May to early September	Early June to early August
Muirtown	1415	1015	1900
Dochgarroch	1500	1100	1945
Tor Point	1530	1130	2015
Urquhart Castle	1600	—	—
Tor Point	1630	1130	2015
Dochgarroch	1700	1200	2045
Muirtown	1745	1245	2130

Inanimate objects as sources of deception. As Baker has observed, at a suitable distance and under appropriate lighting conditions all inanimate objects can become most convincing 'monsters', although optical enlargement can usually reveal the true nature of the objects.[19] Again the objects may be either natural or man-made. The commonest natural inanimate objects are floating logs or tree trunks. In 1960 Baker's expedition was misled by a floating fir tree,[20] and Dinsdale's first glimpse of N turned out to be a tree.[21] Gould told how a log, brought down the River Moriston by a spate, drifted out from its mouth and went ashore on the west side of Invermoriston Pier. Some observers were certain that it was N.[22] E. Montgomery Campbell records an incident in Urquhart Bay where a log deceived a large group of people, including herself.[23]

Vegetable mats are another natural source of deception. It has been established that in some lakes rotting vegetation on the bottom will spontaneously rise to the surface as a result of gas production within it. One such incident was fortuitously photographed on L Lochy, and this phenomenon has been observed on Norwegian lakes, where it appears to have been the result of sawmill operations. Burton has explored this as an explanation for reports of N, where logs or branches in the mat could be mistaken for N's head and/or neck.[24] Such mats can only rise from relatively shallow areas of L Ness.

Partly submerged rocks were listed by Baker as one inanimate source of deception, but in L Ness these occur only near the shore where observers can see what they are (although Binns appears to have found one out from the shore[25]).

Although there have been some reports of oil drums floating on L Ness, the principal man-made inanimate source of deception is a boat. Baker stated that boats can be most deceptive, and that at a distance of 1.5 km or more a 4.5 m rowing boat often appears as a dark 'blob' (although binoculars could identify it). However, a small outboard motor boat at a similar distance could be more difficult to identify. He suggested that such craft, wandering in and out of the bays along the lake, were responsible for many reports of N.[26] After an experience at Foyers in 1960, Burton discovered that such powered boats certainly are mistaken for N.[27]

Animal sources of deception. Among the sources considered by Baker were fish, birds, and mammals. Although fish are unlikely to cause deception above water, geese and diving birds can deceive. Geese swimming in line astern make a perfect many-humped N, and a black-throated diver, partially submerged and swimming at speed, leaving a noticeable wake, fits the preconceived idea of N in all respects but size (itself difficult to judge). Baker and Westwood noted that the deception is most marked when the birds take off and fly close to the water, beating the surface with their wing tips. They become a series of humps, shrouded in spray, speeding across the water and leaving behind them a wake much larger than one would expect.[28] Alex Campbell admitted that he had been deceived by a flock of cormorants.[29]

The only mammalian sources of deception are deer, seals and otters. Deer are not afraid of water and will swim quite wide lakes. Burton drew attention to the fact that a swimming and submerged deer is not always recognised as such, and he cited an example. In its second year of life, the red deer carries a pair of short unbranched antlers, and during July and August these are in velvet (covered in fur). The antlers swell slightly at the tips and look just like two short horns.[30] Seals occasionally enter L Ness but they are usually easily identified, and the last one to do so was shot after only a few months.

While it is agreed that otters do inhabit L Ness, the questions of whether or not they are mistaken for N, and if so to what extent, are controversial. In 1815 Sir Walter Scott noted that 'an otter swimming seems a very large creature', and suggested this explanation for the monster long reported to inhabit Cauldshields L near his home, Abbotsford.[31] Baker and Westwood were once misled by an otter, and Costello admits that otters may account for some reports of lake monsters. A 'monster' seen struggling in L Arkaig by four men in a pinnace was later identified by the stalker who accompanied them as an otter.[32] The notion that otters are rarely seen in L Ness begs the question of whether or not the average observer can identify the animal. Knowledge of otters is not widespread, certainly not among urbanites. The Highlands is a last refuge for an animal that has been largely exterminated in Southern Britain, but even countrymen see little of it. It keeps out of the way of humans, and is very shy. In consequence, few people, on coming across an otter, recognise it. Otters can swim at a speed of up to 3 m/s, perhaps faster in a sprint, and they can run faster than a man on land. They can remain submerged for 3–4 min. and, consequently, can swim underwater for a distance up to 700 m (half the width of L Ness). The European otter can dive to a depth of 15 m, and may be able to dive deeper. Otters up to 2 m long (including the tail) have been found, some in the L Ness area. Their fur is brown, paler underneath, with white patches on cheeks and throat. They are playful and will often twist and turn at the surface, throwing their tails into the air. They can also tread water so as to make a 'long neck', where the head and neck project straight up out of the water as they survey their surroundings. If disturbed away from the water, an otter will instinctively make for it, even crossing a road to do so.[33]

Relative frequency of sources of deception. The only data on relative frequency is Baker and Westwood's observation that of 16 mistakes on their 1962 expedition, 8 were wake effects, 6 were birds, one was an otter, and one a salmon (in fact the remaining two were probably otters). Small as this sample is, it shows the predominance of wave-wake deceptions, and it is important to note their comment that only the wake effects compared in size with the 'huge manifestations' of the 1930s. Despite this it may be that the humble otter has been responsible for more reports than is generally recognised.

The Evidence from Other Lakes

L Ness is not the only lake supposed to contain large aquatic animals; a similar tradition is connected with many other Scottish lakes, besides lakes in other temperate regions of the world. In chapter 7 I shall review the evidence for the existence of some of these creatures. However, conclusions are necessarily dependent on the conclusions regarding N which, as the archetype, can be taken for the class of creatures with which we are concerned. Belief in many of these other creatures is clearly influenced by belief in N, indeed it may have been created by the fame of N. Consequently our conclusions regarding N may be taken as conclusions about the existence of any or all lake-creatures.

Arrangement of the Evidence

Mackal concluded that the evidence falls naturally into four categories: (1) visual observations; (2) still photographs; (3) motion picture film;

and (4) sonar contacts, and that each of these classes of evidence is qualitatively different.[34] It can be argued that there are only two qualitatively different classes of evidence, that from eyewitnesses and that from instruments. The instrumental evidence can be subdivided according to the instrument and/or the method in which it is used. I shall deal with the evidence in the following categories:

(1) the eyewitness evidence
(2) the above-water photographic evidence (still and cine)
(3) the underwater photographic evidence (all still)
(4) the sonar evidence (including a note on radar evidence).

Although there have been attempts to obtain other sorts of evidence (remains, tracks, tissue samples, or even a live specimen), none has been successful.

2

The Eyewitness Evidence

Unlike evidence from instruments, evidence from witnesses is subject to several processes which we tend to overlook. First the witnesses must perceive the event which interests us. Later they must use memory recall to relate the event. Much can go wrong with either or both of these processes.

Human perception is a complex activity of the brain, and we do not necessarily perceive in the brain what we perceive with our sense organs. The brain is prone to guesswork and it may determine what we see from scraps of information and from what it is expecting. Thus we cannot always accept that witnesses actually saw what they tell us they saw. Generally it is found that a witness embroiders a simple occurrence. In the case of L Ness, as we have seen, there are many stimuli which could cause someone who expects to see N to do so. In fact most visitors to L Ness, and not a few of the natives, expect to see N.

Perception involves estimation of size, distance and speed, and it is well known that few can make accurate estimates of these parameters, especially without a frame of reference. According to Mackal, estimates of the size of unknown objects on water by untrained observers vary from exactly right to 3–5 times too great,[35] and in tests he found that estimates of speed ranged from correct to five times too great.[36] Generally there is a tendency for observers to exaggerate both size and speed.

Visual perception involves eyesight, the quality of which is rarely questioned. In only one case have I seen any mention of the strength, let alone the existence, of a witness's spectacles.[37]

To report a sighting a witness must also use memory, a faculty which is not always reliable. All people include an inventive, imaginative (and therefore spurious) element in their remembering, and all remembering depends heavily on reconstruction rather than on mere reproduction alone.[38] Buckhout has shown how unreliable eyewitness testimony can be, and how the witness may have trouble separating fact from fiction.

The witness may not have been paying much attention, the event may have been too short, or the viewing conditions may have been poorer than the witness allowed.[39] Tests show that unreliability increases with time, and it is strongly suspected that witnesses attempt to make facts fit theory. In the case of N, the theory is pretty well defined and capable of exerting a powerful influence on all who report it.

Finally it should be remembered that not everyone is honest. Some of the eyewitness reports may be deliberate deception (there is plenty of published material on which to base such a deception), and some will come from people whose mental health is poor.

Overall, human beings are not the careful and reliable observers that they are often taken to be.

Number of Eyewitness Reports

According to Mackal there are at least 10,000 known *reported* sightings at L Ness, but less than a third of these are *recorded*. He does not justify this claim, but he does claim to have evaluated almost 3000 published reports. Of these he lists 251 'valid observations' having excluded reports that 'seemed clearly to be waves, birds, logs and other such known objects' or, as in the case of three reports, made by persons showing signs of mental disorder.[40] It is a problem to know how to deal with these reports; they vary greatly in scope and content. Mackal's chronological list is not very helpful, although he did attempt to draw conclusions via the parameters of time, location, duration, weather and surface conditions, range, tail head-neck, body, colour and texture, and motion. However, it is a mistake to assume that all 251 reports refer to the same phenomenon. As the previous chapter has shown there are very many phenomena that a witness can mistake for N, and very little examination of the reports is needed before the conclusion is reached that many of them relate to known phenomena. Indeed, it would be unscientific to exclude the possibility that all reports are of known phenomena.

I propose to consider the witnesses' reports according to the known phenomenon which could account for each report. I shall then ask whether or not the phenomena really do account for the reports. Naturally I cannot discuss all reports, not even Mackal's 251, but I shall try to deal with the more famous ones. Mackal's first report (surprisingly) is that attributed to St Columba. This report is in a class by itself.

Mythological Reports

In his biography of St Columba (written about AD 665), the then Abbot of Iona (Adomnan or Eonan) described how the saint triumphed over a 'water beast' in the River Ness. He claimed that Columba's word prevented 'the savage beast' from biting a swimmer.[41] It has been suggested that this is the earliest record of N.

The episode forms part of a collection of stories demonstrating the saint's power over animals; it is preceded by a story of his power over a wild boar and followed by an account of how he neutralised the poison of snakes. Grimshaw and Lester claim that Adomnan's purpose was to show that the saint and his religion were more powerful than the religion of the native pagan culture. Since this latter culture was largely based on worship of elements associated with water, domination of a water beast (even if it had never been seen) subsumed domination of the culture based on them.[42] It seems more likely that Adomnan's purpose was to demonstrate that even the animals which were worshipped by the Picts were controlled by the power of Christianity. Although the events related by Adomnan may be true, he had powerful reasons for inventing them and persuading pagans that they must convert to his religion. Since he was writing of events that were alleged to have occurred a century before, hardly anyone could have challenged his account; but today we can see that it was probably all invention. There are no modern reports of N attacking human beings, or of it behaving in the manner described by Adomnan. Clearly he invented the account from what was believed at the time (that N lived in L Ness and that it was the cause of drownings). Binns gives many other reasons for not taking Adomnan seriously.[43] In a circular argument Joyce has used the modern reports of N to justify acceptance of Adomnan's story.[44]

That the event was placed in the River Ness has been taken as reason enough to dissociate the event from N. However, there was a major crossing at Bona Narrows, between L Ness and L Dochfour, where (before the canal was built) the waterway became a short river. This may be where Adomnan placed the incident.

Wave-like Reports

It is sometimes difficult to distinguish between the types of wave that may be responsible for the reports, between breaking waves and 'standing waves'. But the following may be an example of a soliton.

Alex Campbell of Fort Augustus was out rowing in his boat opposite the Horseshoe (Scree) on a 'beautiful' (calm?) summer day in 1955 or 1956 when the boat suddenly started to heave underneath him. He was terrified. The boat seemed to rise and then stagger back almost immediately.[45]

Other reports are explicable as solitons breaking in shallows. In 1926 Simon Cameron was watching two gulls skimming the surface near Cherry Island when the gulls suddenly rose screaming into the air.

Then something like a large upturned boat rose from the depths with water cascading down its sides. Just as suddenly, it sank out of sight.[46] At about 8.15 p.m. on 22 July 1930 three young anglers (one was Ian Milne who later kept a gunsmith's shop in Inverness) were fishing in a dead calm off Tor Point near Dores when they heard a great noise and saw much commotion in the water about 600 m away down the lake (southwards). This commotion, throwing spray up into the air, advanced to within 300 m of their boat and then seemed to turn aside into the bay above Dores. Their boat rocked violently as a 75 cm-high wave passed. They claimed that although they detected a wriggling motion, the wash hid the 'creature' from view. Milne stated that the object travelled at a speed of 7 m/s with an undulating motion; he compared it to an enormous conger eel, and was sure that it was neither a seal nor an otter.[47] Colonel Patrick Grant was driving north out of Fort Augustus (past Cherry Island) at about midday on 13 November 1951 when he saw a great disturbance in the water about 150 m from the shore. About 2 m of some black object was showing about 30 cm out of the water, but as he looked it disappeared only to reappear a moment later at least 100 m away and nearer the shore. The speed of movement was very great.[48] Just before his retirement, Alex Campbell claimed to have seen N as he was passing Cherry Island. He saw just one hump about 2.4 m long and half as high which 'shot off' to the other side of the lake at a great speed leaving a large wash.[49]

Apart from waves breaking in the shallows at the north and south ends of L Ness, there have been many reports of what seem to be such waves breaking in Urquhart Bay. At about 4.15 p.m. on 30 July 1979 art

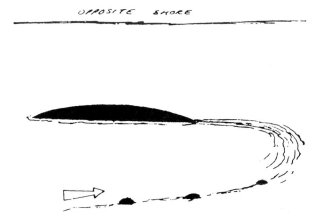

Fig. 1: Alastair Boyd's sketch of the phenomenon he saw in Urquhart Bay. The view is from above Temple Pier.

teachers Alastair and Sue Boyd noticed a small, dark shape appear and disappear three times very quickly. It was moving into the Bay about 150 m from the shore. The object then seemed to churn about in a left turn and surface a little further away looking like the top of a huge tyre inner tube (see Fig. 1). It was visible for only about 5 seconds.[50]

Subsequent tests showed that there was no reason to doubt Alastair's estimate that the hump was 6 m long. At about the same time on 31 August 1979 Muriel Clark and Isobel MacLeod were passing Temple Pier when they noticed a man studying the water through binoculars. On looking across to the Bay they saw a large disturbance on the surface; huge waves were crashing towards the road. As they stopped the car and got out they saw 'a huge head' and what looked like a coil of a snake, and below the waterline the outline of a huge body. They thought that the 'head' was flat and parallel to the water, large and snake-like. In only a few seconds the phenomenon disappeared, going down 'like a sub-marine'.[51] At about 4 p.m. *Scot II* was due to turn at Urquhart Castle, and in calm water its waves must have broken in Urquhart Bay shortly afterwards.

Many reports appear to be of 'standing waves'. On 24 June 1933 a squad of workmen engaged on blasting operations near Abriachan were startled to see N going up the centre of the lake in the wake of a passing drifter. They said that it had an 'enormous head' and a large heavy body. Even Costello could see that these workmen had mistaken the long rolling wake of the drifter for the humps of N,[52] but a 'standing wave' is more complex than just a wake. On 24 August 1933 three witnesses on the Foyers-Dores road noticed a disturbance on the surface of a very calm L Ness just opposite them and a little over half-way across. A drifter was steaming towards Inverness and the disturbance was some 500 m astern. Since there was calm water between the drifter and the disturbance they concluded that it could not be the wake. There were several humps in line, rising and falling with a slightly undulating motion suggesting a caterpillar. The number of humps and their relative size varied, but they maintained the same speed as the drifter. The humps appeared to create their own wake. Later the witnesses concluded that N had turned around underwater because they thought they saw it going in the opposite direction. Gould later identified the drifter as the *Grant Hay* none of whose crew saw the disturbance.[53] On 20 October that same year, in a calm, *Scot II* was towing (about 73 m astern) a big steel barge (*Muriel*) from Fort Augustus to Inverness. About 5 km up L Ness, when they were travelling at about 5 m/s, engineer Robert MacConnell noticed a wave-like mound of water moving out from the side of the lake until it came in line behind *Muriel*. It then followed the boats until MacConnell shouted to the men on *Muriel*, when it sheared away and disappeared. It was estimated to be about 2.5 m long and 0.5 m high.[54] About 30 August 1938, on a calm L Ness, the steam tug *Arrow* was on her maiden voyage from Leith to Manchester when the captain (Brodie) and mate (Rich) noticed a huge black 'animal' rather like a hump-backed whale emerge on the surface and keep pace with the ship at some distance. The object had two distinct humps, one behind the other, but after a brief disappearance it reappeared with seven humps or coils and tore past the tug 'at a terrific speed', leaving large waves.[55] At 3.15 p.m. on 13 August 1960, the Revd W. L. Dobb and his family had just finished a late lunch at an unknown location beside the lake when they saw large waves moving along on a dead calm surface. It was just as if a motorboat was ploughing through the water, but no boat could be seen. A few seconds later they all saw a large black hump in the middle of the waves, but it quickly disappeared, only to be replaced by two humps.[56] On the evening of 22 June 1993 near Dores, a 'long neck and head' was seen moving about in the water. Edna MacInnes (25) was with her friend David Mackay and her 16-month-old son Arron on the A82 near Abriachan. After watching it for about 10 minutes, they drove around to Dores to get a better look. To their surprise the object was still there. 'We followed it for about 300 feet [91 m]. There was a terrific wake behind it, then suddenly it dived deep with such a splash and disturbance to the calm waters that we had to jump back from the shore to stop getting soaked by its wake'. The object was also seen by James Macintosh and his 13-year-old son James, already at Dores.[56A]

Log-like Reports

In 1960 the story was told of how two local boatmen struggled for hours to land a large catch near Dores. It was never seen or broke water before the line eventually broke. At the time it was thought to be N. Weeks later their minnow was found firmly embedded in a waterlogged tree or pile which blocked the Dochgarroch locks.[57]

Otter-like Reports (in water)

D. Mackenzie of Balnain recalled how when he was on a rock above Abriachan, in October of 1871 or 1872, he saw what he took to be a log of wood coming across the lake. The water was very calm. Instead of going towards the river, as he expected, in the middle it suddenly came to life, looking exactly like an upturned boat, and went at great speed, wriggling and churning up the water, towards Urquhart Castle. He was sure that it was an animal of some sort.[58] About 1889 an Abriachan mason, Alexander Macdonald, who regularly travelled on the mail steamer between Abriachan and Inverness, often claimed to have seen what he called 'the salamander', a strange creature disporting itself on the lake in the early morning. About the same time, Roderick Matheson, part owner of a schooner which frequently made passages along the Caledonian Canal, claimed that, on one of these journeys, he had seen what he described as 'the biggest eel I ever saw in my life'. It had 'a neck like a horse, and a mane somewhat similar'.[59] Some time between 1903 and 1907, John Macleod of Invermoriston, accompanied by a writer from Inverness, was fishing in the pool at the mouth of the River Moriston. Preparing his gear he noticed a large creature lying motionless along the surface on the far side of the pool. After a while he tossed his line in its direction and it made off. He claimed that it was 9–12 m long with a head like an eel and what appeared to be a long tapering tail.[60] An anonymous correspondent to a newspaper wrote of seeing what he took to be a huge seal disporting itself in the River Ness near Ness Castle. It had a huge flat head and a fish in its mouth.[61] A later correspondent, apparently confusing two different accounts, did suggest that the 'seal' was in fact an otter.[62]

The report which sparked off the modern popularity of belief in N probably belongs in this category. In March 1933 John Mackay and his wife, then tenants of the Drumnadrochit Hotel, were returning from Inverness, driving along the old narrow road near the seven-mile stone, opposite Aldourie Castle at the very northern tip of the lake, when Mrs Mackay shouted to her husband to stop and look at an enormous black body rolling up and down. By the time he had stopped the car all he could see were ripples, but he knew that something 'big' was out there, 'about a mile and a half [2.5 km] away' (in fact at that point the lake is only about 1 km wide).[63] According to Gould, Mrs Mackay caught sight of a violent commotion in the mirror-like surface about 100 m from the shore. The commotion subsided and a big wake became visible, apparently caused by something large moving along just below the surface. This wake went away across the water towards Aldourie Pier. Then, about halfway (some 450 m) the cause of the wake emerged, showing as two black humps moving in line, the rear one somewhat larger. They moved forward in a rolling motion like whales or porpoises, but no fins were visible. They rose and sank in an undulating manner. After some time the object turned sharply to port and, after describing a half circle, sank suddenly with considerable commotion.[64]

In June 1937, John MacLean saw an animal less than 20 m away at the mouth of the Alltsigh Burn. First only the head and neck were visible, the latter being over 60 cm long and about 20 cm thick. The head reminded him of that of a sheep, with ears cut off and with a pair of narrow eyes to the front. The animal seemed to be champing away at something and it would throw its head back as if swallowing. After two minutes, it put its head down and a hump and tail came into sight. After submerging it surfaced again further away. He saw no limbs or flippers, but the skin had the appearance of a well-groomed horse – smooth, sleek, and well-polished, dark in colour but fading to a pale straw colour on the belly. He estimated that it was 6 m long and at first he had taken it to be a seal or an otter.[65] The same month two boys from the Abbey School at Fort Augustus (Andrew Smith and Anthony Considine) were on the lake in a small boat. As they looked into the water from the stern they noticed three small creatures swimming away from the stern wash. They were rather like eels except that they had four 'rudimentary' limbs and distinct necks; the boys compared them to large lizards, each about 1 m long. The front limbs were flipper-like and had 'merely a waving motion'; the rear limbs were held close to the body and were used for pushing.[66]

One evening in July 1963, two Dores men (Dan McIntosh and James Cameron) were fishing from a small boat about 200 m off Tor Point. At about 10 p.m. they realised that the boat was rocking on a flat calm water. Suddenly the head and neck of an animal reared 1.2–1.5 m out of the water only 20–30 m away. A short distance behind the neck was a small hump. A moment later it sank vertically, causing a commotion in the water. They continued to fish, but caught nothing. Later McIntosh described the head as wide and ugly and continuous with the curve of the neck. No features were seen on the head, but the brown-black hair formed a mane on the neck.[67]

On the evening of 30 March 1965, a school headmistress and her brother-in-law took a stroll from Dores to Tor Point with the water surface calm and the sun setting over the far end of the lake. Suddenly they saw an animal paddling across the lake towards Dores. It was swimming steadily without splashing, but drawing a visible wake after it. Just about opposite them, the creature turned down the middle of the lake. The head was described as like that of a python, held at right angles to the neck, and about 1.5–2 m out of the water.[68]

At 11.45 a.m. on 10 November 1973, retired farmer Richard Jenkyns, who lived on the lakeside at Invermoriston, started his tractor with such a noise that he frightened some animal into the water with a large splash. At first he saw nothing, but then, about 10–15 m out, he saw a 'fish-like' object starting to appear quite slowly and steadily until it was about 50 cm above the surface. It stayed motionless for a short while, before moving slowly forward and sinking. The colour was black or grey-brown, with a matt texture and what appeared to be scales on the head. Above a long but shut mouth was what appeared to be a small black eye or 'blow hole'. The head profile was like that of a snake.[69]

Otter-like Reports (on land)

As a child, playing in Inchnacardoch Bay during the First World War, Margaret Cameron heard 'crackling' in the trees on the other side of the bay and saw a creature lumber down into the water: 'It had a huge body and its movement . . . was like a caterpillar'. It had shiny skin, the colour of an elephant, and two short round feet at front. After lurching to one side, it put one foot after the other into the water.[70]

One stormy night in February 1919, twelve-year-old Jock Forbes and his farmer father were driving a pony cart home to Foyers near Inverfarigaig when the pony shied and attempted to retreat from something crossing the road about 20 m ahead: 'It came out of the trees above the road, moved slowly across the road and then went down the bank and we heard a splash as, presumably, it went into the water'. Jock thought that the 'beast' was fully the width of the road (about 3 m at that point).[71]

Chauffeur Alfred Cruickshank was driving along the hazardous north bank road about 5 a.m. in April 1923 about 3 km north of Invermoriston. As he crested a small hill his headlamps (dimming because they were powered by a dynamo) illuminated what he thought was a large animal on the outside of a bend about 50 m ahead. 'It had a large humped body standing six feet [1.8 m] high with its belly trailing on the ground and about twelve feet [3.6 m] long, to which was attached a long thick tail which was ten to twelve feet [3–3.6 m] in length. It was moving slowly, sort of waddling away from the road on two legs which I could see on the near side'. He thought he heard a grunting noise. The animal's head was close to its body, with very little neck, and its colour was dark olive to khaki, lighter underneath.[72]

Mr and Mrs F. T. G. Spicer from London were driving between Dores and Foyers at about 4 p.m. on 22 July 1933 when they saw something about 200 m ahead. It was a horizontal, trunk-like object emerging from the bushes above the road, the trunk undulating above the road surface (see Fig. 2). Spicer said,

> It did not move in the usual reptilian fashion but with these arches. The body shot across the road in jerks . . . Although I accelerated towards it, it had vanished by the time we reached the spot . . . I . . . could see where it had gone down through the bracken, but there was no sign of it in the water. The body was about five feet [1.5 m] in height and filled the road . . . I estimated the length to be twenty-five to thirty feet [7–9 m]. Its colour . . . could be called a dark elephant grey. We saw no tail, nor did I notice any mouth on what I took to be the head of the creature. We later concluded that the tail must have been curled around alongside it since there was something protruding above its shoulder which gave the impression that it was carrying something on its back.[73]

Fig. 2: The Spicers' sketch of the animal they saw on the road (as shown by Whyte). A different sketch, less consistent with it being an otter, was shown by Gould and has been reproduced by many other writers.

Spicer's first estimate of length was 2 m but on being told that at that point the road was 3.6 m wide he changed his mind and said that the true length was 7.6 m. Three years later the estimate had become over 9 m, which Costello thought more accurate.[74] The original press report was prefaced by the opinion that the animal was a large otter carrying a young otter in its mouth, and that the appearance of having no feet was due to the speed with which it would scramble rapidly across the road.[75]

In December 1933, Mrs Reid, the wife of the postmaster at Inverfarigaig, was motoring into Inverness when she saw a strange animal lying in a glade on a wooded slope away from the shore. The animal was about 100 m away and partly obscured by bracken. She thought she saw a thick, hairy mane on the neck, and it seemed hairy overall. It was about 2 m long and shaped like a hippopotamus, with a large round head and short thick legs. It was slow moving and dark in colour.[76] In the same area four months earlier near Whitefield, Mrs M. F. MacLennan came across an animal resting on a ledge 2 m above the beach. When she shouted to her family, the animal lurched itself up and slithered over the edge into the water with a splash. She described it as having short, thick clumsy legs, 'with a kind of hoof very like a pig's but much larger', and no ears.[77] Later she compared the 'hoof' with what appeared to be the cloven foot of a dinosaur. She informed Burton, who concluded that it was the foot of an amphibian (e.g. an otter).[78]

At about 1 a.m. on 5 January 1934 W. Arthur Grant, a veterinary student, was riding his motor cycle out from Inverness approaching the Abriachan turn when he noticed something 40 m ahead in the shadows of some bushes on the other side of the road. He was almost upon it when it turned what he thought was a small head on a long neck and made two great bounds across the road and down into the water. He could not see it after that, although there was a great splash. He described the body as 'very hefty' and about 4.5–6 m overall, of which 1.5 m was a 'very powerful' tail. There were two 'front flippers' and two more behind, and the tail, instead of coming to a point, was rounded.[79] Later he described the head as 'rather like a snake or an eel, flat at the top, with a large oval eye'.

One evening at the beginning of February 1934, two young girls from Fort Augustus (Jean MacDonald and Patricia Harvey) were walking along the road less than a kilometre from the town at a spot where the Inchnacardoch Burn runs into the lake. They were startled by the appearance of an animal which crossed the burn on the shore below them and disappeared in the direction of the lake. In a full moon and at a distance of only 20 m they were able to see the creature well enough to give the following description: 2.4–3 m long, with four feet, head about 1.8 m off the ground; thickest part of body appeared to be the shoulder; body tapered considerably towards the tail; very dark in colour but perfectly white under the neck; very short legs but moved rapidly with no noise.[80]

At 6.30 a.m. on 3 June 1934, housemaid Margaret Munro, looking through binoculars towards the beach of Borlum Bay, saw an animal rolling in the sun. It had a 'giraffe-like' neck and an 'absurdly' small head 'out of all proportion to the size of the body' which was dark grey. The underpart of the chest was white and the skin was like that of an elephant. There were two short forelegs or flippers and it was able to arch its back into humps.[81]

Deer-like Reports

Greta Finlay and her son were camping on the south shore 1 km west of Aldourie Castle on 20 August 1952 when, at about noon, her attention was drawn to splashing on the lake shore. Walking around the caravan, she was surprised to see, less than 20 m away, a small 'monster' with a strange head and neck. She told Whyte,

> I was so taken up with the strange appearance of the head and neck that I did not examine the rest of the animal at all closely. There were two or three humps and the total length visible would be about 15 feet [4.5 m]. The neck was held erect, and where it met the water it enlarged to join a bulky body. The head and neck together were 2-2½ feet [60–70 cm] in length, the head alone being about 6 inches [15 cm] long and of about the same width as the neck. What astonished me, apart from the hideous appearance of the head, was that there were two six-inch [15 cm] long projections from it, each with a blob on the end. The skin looked black and shiny and reminded me of a snail more than anything.[82]

Young Finlay made a sketch of the creature (see Fig. 3a); compare it with Burton's sketch (Fig. 3b).

Fig. 3: (a) Top, Harry Finlay's sketch of the animal which frightened him and his mother (drawn two days later); (b) bottom, Burton's sketch, based on photographs and drawn to scale, of a two-year-old red stag deer as it would appear in August and standing or swimming in water. Antlers in velvet and ears back.

Vegetable-mat-like Reports

Several employees of a building contractor and wood merchant watched what they thought was N in Urquhart bay on 15 December 1953. Through binoculars it looked like a huge horse at the front. About 6 m behind there was 'a great splashing', which they took to be the tail. When first seen the forepart was high out of the water and it appeared to shake itself. It disappeared and then reappeared but moved out of range of vision.[83] At an unidentified location (perhaps Borlum Bay) a 'brownish drab-coloured hump' rose out of the water 40 m from the shore. It then flattened out, and the process continued until the body assumed the shape of a good-size hump with a smaller hump at each end. Opposite the two latter humps there was continuous 'kicking and splashing' in the water. At the same time a fourth small hump appeared with a water space between it and the other three. Finally this fourth hump was lifted clear and appeared to be the 'head and neck'.[84]

3

The Above-water Still Photographic Evidence

The first report of an attempt to photograph N was in August 1933 when a well-known photographer, Captain Ellisford, arrived with a large box of 'modern' photographic materials, including a telephoto lens; nothing more was heard of him. The first record of anyone attempting to photograph what they took to be N was that describing how the Revd N. Dundas who, with his wife, claimed to have seen N from Temple Pier at Drumnadrochit on 23 November 1933. However, N did not appear in his photograph.[85]

I know of 21 photographs (or sets of photographs) which allege to show N, as shown in Table 2, in which I have followed Mackal's numbering. Comments on individual photographs follow:

Plate II: Hugh Gray's photograph of N (*Fortean Picture Library; copyright expired*).

P1: 12 November 1933 by Hugh Gray. This photograph (see Plate II) was the first which alleged to show N. Gray was an employee of the British Aluminium Company at the factory in Foyers. He made the following statement:

> Four Sundays ago, after church, I went for my usual walk near where the Foyers river enters the loch. The loch was like a mill pond and the sun was shining brightly. An object of considerable dimensions rose out of the water not so very far from where I was. I immediately got my camera ready and snapped the object which was then two or three feet [0.75 m] above the surface of the water. I did not see any head, for what I took to be the front parts were under water, but there was considerable movement from what seemed to be the tail, the part furthest from me. The object only appeared for a few minutes then sank out of sight.[86]

Apparently Gray took five pictures of the object, but four were blank. Then the film was left in a drawer for three weeks before his brother

Table 2:
List of alleged above-water still photographs of N

No.	Date	Photographer	Location
P1	12 Nov 1933	Hugh Gray	Foyers
P2+	19 Apr 1934	Robert Kenneth Wilson	north of Invermoriston
P3	10 Jun 1934	?	near Fort Augustus
P4+	13 Jul 1934°	Team under Sir Edward Mountain	various
P5	24 Aug 1934	E. C. Adams or Dr James Lee	?
P6	14 Jul 1951	Lachlan Stuart	Whitefield
P7	29 Jul. 1955	Peter A. MacNab	Urquhart Castle
P8	1958	H. L. Cockrell	canoe
P9	27 May 1960	Peter O'Connor	near Foyers
P10	22 Jun 1960	Maurice Burton	Foyers
P11	7 Aug 1960	R. H. Lowrie	boat near Aldourie
P12	1964	Peter Hodge	?
P13	20 Aug 1966	Patrick W. Sandemann	?
P14	1967	Peter Dobbie	?
P15+	21 Oct 1972*	Frank Searle	?
P18	5 Oct 1975	Alan Wilkins	Rubha Ban
P19+	21 May 1977	Anthony Nicol Shiels	Urquhart Castle
P20	1981	Alexander Williams	boat
P21	1982	Jennifer Bruce	Temple Pier

Notes:

P16/17 are Rines's 1972 and 1975 photographs, which are dealt with in chapter 5.

+ denotes that more than one photograph is referred to by this number.

° The beginning of one month's observation during which time the photographs were taken.

* several photographs attributed to this date and some to subsequent dates.

took it for development and printing.[87] He explained to Gould that he had not taken the film for immediate processing because he thought that he had 'probably missed the creature altogether'.[88]

The picture and Gray's story were published in various newspapers on 6 December 1933 together with a statement by Kodak staff that the negative had not been tampered with. Despite this a contributor to *Nature* in 1933 noted that there seemed to be indications that it was not a direct contact print from an untouched negative. More recently Dinsdale has expressed the view that either the print has been 'touched up' or light has spoiled the picture.[89] On the other hand, four photographic experts consulted by Burton all pronounced it to be 'without trace of tampering'.[90] The original negative is lost, but two copy negatives have been discovered.

Binns took comparative photographs from the 'same spot, although it is not known how this spot was identified, and was surprised at the absence of shoreline and foliage in P1.[91] The geometry of the picture indicates that the camera was at an angle of about 12° to the plane of the water, and that Gray was much closer to the object than he admitted. In this case the object is smaller than N; Burton was sure that it shows an otter rolling at the surface.[92] It has been suggested that the picture shows a Labrador dog swimming towards the camera with a stick in its mouth, and indeed this interpretation can be seen in P1. An attempt to clarify the image by use of a digital processing technique was not successful.

P2: 19 April 1934 by Robert Kenneth Wilson. This picture (see Plate III) is the famous 'Surgeon's Photograph'. Wilson was a London gynaecologist on holiday with a friend. They were motoring to Inverness and had stopped for a break about 4 km north of Invermoriston on the road beside L Ness. At that time the road had not been improved. With him Wilson had a quarter-plate camera with a telephoto lens, but it is not clear whether or not he was hunting N. In a contemporary newspaper report, he said that he took it 'in the hope that I would see the monster', but in a letter to Whyte 21 years later he said that the camera was for photographing wild fowl and trains. There is also conflict as to whether the camera was his or whether he borrowed it (which has a bearing on how skilled he was in its use). In 1934 he stated that he took the camera out of the car and had it ready with him 'in case I should spy the monster'; in 1955 he declared that he rushed back to the car to get the camera after seeing N. In 1934 he gave the time as midday; in 1955 it was between 7 and 7.30 a.m.

In 1955 he claimed that he was at a point where the road was 'some hundred feet [30 m]' above the water, but that in 1954 he had been unable to locate the exact spot 'within a mile'. Suddenly he noticed a

Plate III: Part of R. K. Wilson's first photograph of N (*Associated Newspapers; copyright expired*).

commotion in the water 'between 150 and 200 yards [137–183 m] from the shore' (1934) or 'two or three hundred yards [183–275 m] out' (1955), where 'the head of some strange animal' rose up out of the water. He managed to take four photographs before the object sank from view, but two showed nothing when they were developed and printed by an Inverness chemist. The best picture (Plate III) was assigned to *The Daily Mail*, who published it with Wilson's account on 21 April 1934. The chemist kept a copy negative of this picture (although both it and the original are lost) together with a print of the second picture (see Plate IV), which passed to Whyte who first published it. Wilson, who died in Australia in 1969, never claimed to have photographed N; he merely claimed to have photographed an object moving in L Ness. He shunned all publicity and refused to discuss the picture with the press.

Explanations for the object have included a large tree root brought to the surface by convection currents or gas bubbles (Linnean Society), a diving bird, such as a crested grebe (accepted by Mackal[93]), the pectoral fin of a 'sick pilot whale',[94] and the tail of an otter (Burton[95]).

Plate IV: Part of R. K. Wilson's second photograph of N (*author's collection: copyright expired*).

Assuming that the second photograph not only shows the same object as that in the first photograph but that it was taken immediately afterwards, Witchell argued that there would not have been time to catch a swinging otter's tail on both pictures. However, as Burton has pointed out, it is not certain that the two photographs do show the same obect, and, in any case, they do not seem to be taken at the same angle or in the same surface conditions. If the first shows an otter's tail, the second seems to show its head!

Although both Dinsdale and Holiday attempted analysis of the first picture, neither realised that the ripple rings allow the angle of the camera to the water to be calculated. This angle turns out to be about 19°, which, if Wilson was 30 m above the water, means that the object was about 95 m away, much less than even his 1934 estimate. In fact he could not have been 30 m above L Ness.

Between Invermoriston and Alltsigh the old road was between 26 and 30 m above the water at several points, but after the second milestone (3.2 km) the road fell to within 9 to 12 m high. (The present A82 follows roughly the same course.) However, trees hid the water (as they do now) for most of the way at the high level. The only gap is just short of the second milestone, where there is a field between the road and the shore (although there are trees along the shore). Unfortunately geometry shows that Wilson could not have taken the picture from anywhere in this field; at the top of the field the object distance is *less* than the distance between the camera and the shore, and the further down the field Wilson stood, the nearer the object must have been. In fact the first picture, having no foreground, cannot have been taken from this field.

Picture analysis shows that the bottom of the picture subtends an angle of 35° to the horizontal without showing any shore. To obtain this Wilson must have stood on that part of the road which is only about 10 m above L Ness (or even nearer and lower on the shore). In this case the object was only 30 m from the camera and only about 70 cm high. This size is consistent with it being the tail of an otter. The shape is also consistent with this explanation. For many years there has been a rumour in the Wilson family that the picture was a hoax.

The Loch Ness Centre at Drumnadrochit displays some digitised reconstructions of the picture made by Alan Gillespie at JPL in Pasadena. Because these were not produced from the negative they show no more than can be seen in the available prints; in fact, due to the reproduction process, they show more than was in the original (the impression of whiskers). Witchell's claim that the picture was enhanced[96] is not true.[97]

In 1994, David Martin and Alastair Boyd claimed that the photograph was taken for the noted hoaxer Marmaduke Wetherell by his son Ian. They alleged that the object was actually a toy submarine modified by the addition of a head and neck made of plastic wood and weighted with lead ballast. The model was floated in 'a quiet bay' on L Ness, and sunk when a water bailiff approached.[97A] As unlikely as this seems, Martin and Boyd traced Christian Spurling, then 89, and Wetherell's stepson, who admitted making the model and participating in the hoax. Spurling died just four months later. It was alleged that the pictures were transferred to plates and that Col. Wilson was persuaded to take them for development in Inverness by a mutual friend.[266]

F. David Crump was sceptical that a model submarine would support the extra weight and Richard Smith drew attention to the analysis by LeBlond and Collins, which showed the 'neck' to be 1.2 m high; he also referred to the second picture,[97B] which may in fact show the model sinking

P6: 14 July 1951 by Lachlan Stuart. Stuart was employed by the Forestry Commission in clearing timber on the south side of the Dores–Foyers road and lived in a house called Whitefield with his wife and children and lodger Taylor Hay, also a forester.

He stated that when he rose at 6.20 a.m. to milk his cow he saw what he thought was a boat speeding along the middle of the lake towards Dores, but he thought it was travelling too fast for a boat. Then, seeing humps, he concluded that it was N 'which has been [seen] several times in this vicinity this week'. He shouted to his wife, and to Hay, grabbed the camera, and hurried down to the shore. By this time, apparently, N had made a U-turn and was travelling towards Foyers about 45 m offshore. Displaying three humps, and a long thin neck which repeatedly ducked underwater, it appeared to be making for a point on the shore about 36 m away. He photographed it as it passed him (see Plate V). He claimed that all the humps were about 1.5 m across at the base and between 60 and 120 cm out of the water. He alleged that, after the picture had been taken, N approached to within about 4.5 m of the shore, causing Hay and himself to retreat to the trees from where they saw N turn with a great splashing and make off towards the centre of the lake. When it was about 275 m out, it submerged, never to reappear.[98]

Plate V: Part of Lachlan Stuart's photograph of N (*author's collection; copyright Lachlan Stuart*).

The newspaper which published Stuart's story and picture arranged for the film to be developed and printed by commercial photographer John Macpherson of Drumcharrel, Cawdor, Nairn. He stated that the film appeared to be perfectly normal and that the low light level was consistent with the picture being taken at 6.30 a.m. The negative development took nearly twice the normal time.

Brendan Kemmet and John Quigley of the paper spent three days at L Ness testing the story and hoping to discover that Stuart was a practical joker interested in trick photography. They found that the picture had been taken with a primitive box camera which actually belonged to Elsie Stuart. In fact Stuart had to get his wife to load and unload it for him. In addition, the faulty winding mechanism could only be operated by Elsie. The picture of N was the sixth of eight, the previous five pictures being of Elsie and the children. After photographing N, Stuart did not immediately despatch the film for development, and Elsie took two further pictures around the house. In fact the film might still be lying in the camera if the newspaper had not heard a rumour that such a photograph existed. They had sent George Paterson, their chief Inverness representative, to collect the spool. Stuart stated that he had intended to take the spool to a chemist 'to see if I had really managed to get the monster's picture'.

Stuart, who had an excellent reputation and had worked for the Commission for fifteen years, was questioned by Kemmet and Quigley for two days. They examined the camera, the negative and the spot where the picture was taken. They also took comparison photographs. Step by step they traced the headlong rush to the lakeside. But they could shake the testimony of neither man, nor could they find any flaw in the story or the evidence. Their verdict was that the picture was not faked or 'stunted'; and that both men were sincere in their story. Stuart swore 'All I have told you – and I've told you it over and over again – is the solemn truth'. Neither man owned a boat, nor were there any boats around that part of the lake.[99]

Recent attempts to trace Stuart have failed. The Forestry Commission have no record of him, even though the cottage at Whitefield was owned by them in 1951, and was let to 'L. Stuart'. However, by 1952 he was no longer there.

Burton, who spoke to Stuart in September 1951, concluded that this is the 'most important photograph'.[100] Mackal also regarded the photograph as of 'considerable importance' and thought that it showed three N together.[101] Binns noted the immobility of the humps, and also that they are out of alignment. He thought that they were too close to the shore in shallow water, implying that they were rocks, a sample of which he photographed.[102]

Making certain assumptions about the camera, it can be shown that if the objects are in the water they are about 21 m away and about 6 m long overall. From the fact that the camera was aimed at Urquhart Castle we know that it was pointed at about 45° to the shore; this puts the nearest object to the shore still 11 m from it. At that distance the water is too deep for it to be a rock.

Since the picture was taken looking south-west, the sun, which appears to be in the top right-hand corner of the (uncropped) picture, cannot be rising. The picture was taken, not in the early morning as Stuart stated, but in the late evening. Only in the late '80s was it revealed that Stuart had, at the time, admitted to a local resident (author Richard Frere) that the humps were constructed of bales of hay covered with tarpaulins.[102A] So was 'Taylor Hay', code for 'a tale of hay'?

Plate VI: Peter MacNab's photograph of N (*author's collection; copyright P. A. MacNab*).

P7: 29 July 1955 by Peter A. MacNab. After they had previously published P8, *The Weekly Scotsman*, on 23 October 1958, published a photograph (Plate VI) and an account sent in by MacNab, an Ayrshire councillor and bank manager. He explained the delay as being due to 'diffidence and fear of ridicule'. Witchell obtained the following account:

> I was returning from a holiday in the north with my son and pulled the car up on the road just above Urquhart Castle. It was a calm, warm hazy afternoon. I was all ready to take a shot of Urquhart Castle when my attention was held by a movement in the calm water over to the left.

Naturally I thought of the 'Monster' and hurriedly changed over the standard lens of my Exacta (127) camera to a six-inch [150 mm] telephoto. As I was doing so a quick glance showed that some black or dark enormous water creature was cruising on the surface.

Without a tripod and in a great hurry I took the shot. I also took a very quick shot with another camera, a fixed-focus Kodak, before the creature submerged.

My son was busy under the bonnet of the car at the time and when he looked in response to my shouts there were just ripples on the water. Several cars and a bus stopped but they could see nothing and listened to my description with patent disbelief.

So great was the scepticism and leg-pulling by friends to whom he showed the picture that in a fit of exasperation he threw away the second negative (the one taken with the Kodak?).[103]

MacNab lent Mackal what the former termed 'the original negative', but Mackal claimed that a print made from this negative differed markedly from a version of the photograph published by Whyte in 1957 (*sic*).[104]

The differences are accounted for, as Mackal guessed, only by supposing that a print has been rephotographed inexpertly. This discovery caused Mackal to reject the photograph as evidence for N, although his reasoning is unclear.[105]

Burton identified the object as a stern wave from a ship that had passed a short while before,[106] and Binns suggested that it was the wake from three trawlers travelling closely together towards Fort Augustus.[107] The picture does show faint traces of a wake further out from and parallel to the object which is alleged to be N.

P8: 1958 by H. L. Cockrell. During the late summer Cockrell spent several days paddling about in a canoe with a specially rigged flash camera attached to his life-jacket. Just about dawn after his final night operation he noticed something about 45 m away which seemed to be swimming steadily towards him. It looked like a very large flat head about 1.5 m long and wide, with a wash about 1 m behind. Convinced that it was N he photographed it, after which a light squall blew up. At this the object seemed to sink but after the squall he could still see something on the surface. This turned out to be a long stick about 2.5 cm thick. Cockrell's conviction that he had photographed a stick changed when he saw the picture. It seemed to show more than just a stick (although it is hard to say what it shows).[108]

Mackal was content to accept that it was only a stick and that Cockrell's fatigue led him to see it as something else,[109] and Lehn has proposed that atmospheric refraction caused Cockrell to see the stick as N.[110]

P9: 27 May 1960 by Peter O'Connor. Described by Binns as 'a publicity-seeking twenty-six-year-old Gateshead fireman',[111] O'Connor, with a companion, camped on the shore near Foyers for a few days. He claimed that, awakened at about 6 a.m., he noticed N gliding around a headland at the speed of a fast walking pace. He waded out into the water, waist deep, and snapped a picture with his flash, turned to shout at his companion, and then snapped a second picture without flash. He claimed to have been within 25 m of the animal, and stated that it had small sheep-like features set on very strong neck muscles, which kept rippling. He judged the head to be about 25 cm long, while the neck was about 150 cm in diameter, increasing in thickness, with about 70 cm visible. He saw no eyes, but indicated that its facial structure suggested that it had them, but that its 'lids' were shut. The 'hump' or body was smooth, grey-black, about 5 m long at the waterline, with about 1 m of water separating neck and body.[112] The camera was a Brownie Flash 20, set at f/14, and 0.02 s. Film was Ilford HP3 and flash bulbs were Photoflux PF5.

P9 was published on 16 June 1960, just before Burton and his team arrived at Foyers. Naturally it was discussed among the guests at the hotel, some suggesting that it was a half-submerged but inflated sack. Burton ignored the picture, which he thought unconvincing, but the gillie who took him and his family out in his motorboat for occasional excursions insisted on taking them to what he called 'O'Connor's Cove'. On landing they found abundant signs that someone had camped there; ashes from a fire lay about and a bivouac had been made by tying down the lower branches of a small tree with an unusual kind of red-and-white string. There were used flash bulbs and charred fragments of what must have been several white plastic sacks. One of the party, who had decided to paddle in the shallows, tripped over some red-and-white string (the same) which turned out to be attached to half a dozen rocks each about 25 cm across and forming a circle about 1 m in diameter. It was clear that someone had inflated a plastic sack and weighted it around the edge with stones. The head and neck of the 'monster' had consisted of a stick which Burton and his party missed because it was lying in the bivouac, but it was discovered shortly afterwards by retired journalist Angus Forbes. Unfortunately the stick was lost when Forbes attempted a reconstruction of the model.[113]

Dinsdale, who at first accepted O'Connor's story and published it, removed it from subsequent editions of his book after Mackal and Witchell had expressed doubts. In fact Mackal has rejected it as evidence.[114]

P10: 22 June 1960 by Maurice Burton. Although Mackal lists this as a picture of N, it is merely a picture of some ripples seen by Burton and his team at Foyers. Burton did not present it as N, although he could not identify its cause. The ripples were probably caused by an otter swimming just under the surface.

P11: 7 August 1960 by R. H. Lowrie. The Lowrie family were aboard the yacht *Finola* near Dores when, at 4.15 p.m., they noticed 'a curious form' coming up astern between 3 and 5 m/s looking like 'a couple of ducks, occasionally submerging, and a neck-like protrusion breaking the surface'. After about 10 minutes it swung away to starboard towards Aldourie Point (location uncertain) and some photographs were taken. It moved quickly causing considerable disturbance and showing a large area of green and brown. Since it seemed to be heading directly towards them they decided to alter course to avoid a collision. They estimated the object's length as that of their boat, 12 m. The photograph shows very little except two long lines of wave. According to Witchell the object was also seen by a party on the shore.[115]

P13: 20 August 1966 by Patrick W. Sandemann. Only Mackal has published and referred to this picture.[116] It shows a V-wash moving directly away from the camera on a very calm surface.

P15: 21 October 1972 to 26 February 1976 by Frank Searle. Many pictures alleged to show N have been produced by Searle, a retired greengrocer from London, who camped beside the lake first at Balachladaich and later on Foyers pier from 1969 to 1983. No doubt frustrated by N's non-appearance he resorted to photographing models and logs which he presented as pictures of N. Later he began to photograph pieces of a picture of a brontosaurus stuck on to watery backgrounds. These too were presented as genuine pictures of N. Searle is now totally discredited and has left L Ness.[117]

P18: 18 July 1975 by Alan Wilkins. Wilkins was on holiday with his family at a caravan site at Rubha Ban, near Invermoriston. The water was flat calm and he and his son were on watch with still and cine cameras at the ready by 6.25 a.m. At 7.20 a.m. a long dark line appeared in mid-lake off a point 3.5 km to the north-east. It sank slowly, only to reappear several more times, the last of which was photographed twice. Through binoculars Wilkins thought that he could make out a large black shape rising out of the water in the same area. It seemed to be of great size, and as it sank back again after only a few seconds' exposure with water swirling at its base, suggested a bulky body below. After a further appearance as a long line, it was suddenly gone.

For the rest of that day, Wilkins and the occupants of the adjoining caravan saw mysterious objects on the water, and photographed some of them. These latter photographs have not been published.

Wilkins used a Canon 35 mm SLR type FTB camera connected via an adapter and a Novoflex focusing bellows to a Novoflex 640 mm telephoto lens.

David James arranged for the pictures to be developed and printed and then submitted them to Sir Peter Scott and Richard Fitter. It was reported that the films were to be examined by JARIC and also that they were to be computer enhanced at JPL in Pasadena.[118] Nothing has been heard from either JARIC or JPL, and although Wilkins sent the original negatives to the Academy of Applied Science (AAS) he has had neither a reply nor return of any film.

Plate VII: A. N. Shiels's first photograph of N (*Fortean Picture Library; copyright A. N. Shiels*).

P19: 21 May 1977 by Anthony Nicol Shiels. Self-styled 'wizard and professional psychic' (referred to by Dinsdale as a 'professional artist and showman'), Shiels (also known as 'Doc') alleged to have photographed N from Urquhart Castle at 4 p.m. He had been sitting in the Castle grounds when 'suddenly up popped a head and neck about 100 yards [91 m] away'. Apparently no-one else saw this event, and yet Shiels had time to snatch two pictures with his 35 mm SLR camera (fitted with a 135 mm lens) (see Plates VII and VIII).

Shiels alleged that about 1.5 m of N was visible. He said:

> Don't take any notice of what appear to be eyes . . . I could see no eyes as such in the original. The light patch above the mouth (if mouth it is, and I think it is) is merely a reflection of a kind of ridge . . . Skin texture, smooth and glossy. The animal was visible for no more than 4–6 seconds. It held itself very upright, very still, except for a turning of the head and a straightening of the back . . . It had powerful neck muscles. There is . . . possible evidence of a parasitic growth at the back of the neck, on the dorsal ridge, as a pale yellow-green patch is visible near the water. Also in both pictures, a round pale object floats on the water close to the neck.

Plate VIII: An enlargement from A. N. Shiels's second photograph of N (*Fortean Picture Library; copyright A. N. Shiels*).

Apparently, he thought this pale object was a beer can! Shiels believes that he 'invoked' N just as he 'invoked' Morgawr, the Cornish sea-serpent, by the use of ancient magic and psychic powers and with the aid of a worldwide group of psychics and witches, including his daughters.[119]

An enlarged copy slide of one picture was examined by Ground Saucer Watch (GSW) in Phoenix, Arizona, whose computer analysis techniques have been applied to many UFO photographs. Their conclusions were as follows:

1. Analysis reveals that the wave ripples can be seen through the creature's neck and head, suggesting that it is either transparent or translucent.
2. The image was relatively flat.
3. There is a lack of natural shadows.
4. There is an absence of water displacement.
5. Analysis of wave size and reflection suggests the use of a 300 mm lens.
6. The bright areas on the neck and mouth appear unnatural, as if painted on.
7. There are indications that the image is smaller than apparent size, or further away than estimated.
8. The time and camera direction are confirmed.
9. The photograph shows 'patternized similarity' with others taken in the area.

GSW added that their conclusion (1) could be explained if there had been a double exposure, but that to resolve this they would need to see the original slide.[120]

The accusation that waves could be seen through the image 'dismayed' Shiels; clearly it implied that his N was painted over a watery background. However, others thought the finding proved that the photograph was genuine; it confirmed their belief that N does not inhabit our 'normal' 3D universe.[121]

Dinsdale arranged for the original slide to be examined by Vernon Harrison, ex-President of the Royal Photographic Society. His conclusions were that the slide itself had not been tampered with, that the object was certainly not a common object or a trick of the light, that a long-focus lens had been used, that the course of the neck could be traced for a short distance below the surface of the water, that the reflections were entirely naturalistic, and that 'there is even a wavelet that has been reflected back from the left side of the neck and caught the light of the sun'. Harrison could not say what the image represented, but he did admit that one possible explanation was that it was a hoax – 'a reduction of an imaginative painting executed by a competent artist'. He noted that the artist would require skill and a detailed knowledge of the effects of light reflected from, and transmitted through, rippled water.[122] Photographer Colin Bord also examined the original slide. He thought that the lighting and reflection were entirely consistent with Shiels's report, being particularly impressed by the fact that within the reflection were wavelets reflecting the same blue (sky) as the surrounding water. He was not impressed by the GSW analysis, and found that he could not see the wave ripples through the image. Nor could he imagine Shiels arranging for double exposure or super imposition.[119]

Shiels tells me that he took the pictures from a position at the base of the tower of Urquhart Castle, on the east side facing L Ness. The path around the tower is 7.4 m above the water, so, if Shiels was sitting, the camera would have been about 8 m above the water. Picture analysis and the geometry of the camera combine to show that if the object was in the water at the distance claimed by Shiels then the distant shore of L Ness should show in the picture. That it does not do so means that the object (if really in the water) was not as far away as 91 m (in fact probably only half that distance). I have since concluded that the pictures are fakes, probably made by double exposure.[123]

P20: September, 1981 by Alexander Williams. Williams, a student, was out fishing on L Ness in a flat calm with poor visibility due to mist. The object is alleged to be at 150–200 m range and photographed with a 110 Kodak 'Instamatic'. Hepple obtained a print and an enlargement of P20 from Miles Cato, a fellow-student who claims to own the picture.[124]

P21: 1982 by Jennifer Bruce. On her first holiday to Scotland from Vancouver, Bruce was with her husband Gordon and her mother Norma at Drumnadrochit. Calling for N, she took a picture from Temple Pier looking across to Urquhart Castle. There is no indication that N, or anything else, was in view at the time the picture was taken, but the picture in her photo album now shows what appears to be a sinuous head and neck rearing out of the water (see Plate IX).[125]

Plate IX: Part of Jennifer Bruce's photograph of *N* (*Fortean Picture Library; copyright Jennifer Bruce*).

4

The Above-water Cine and Video Film Evidence

Mackal knew of 22 cine film sequences, which I have used as the basis for Table 3 (q.v.), following his numbering. The amount known about each film varies greatly, and some have been ignored either because of this or because they contain no measurable data.

Cine Film

F1: c. 1935 by Dr McRae. Retired physician Dr McRae spent some time at L Ness in the hope of capturing N on film. It is claimed that just after dawn one morning he came across N floating, apparently asleep, on the surface. He exposed film for four or five minutes. According to the only people to see the film, trustees appointed by Dr McRae, it shows, very clearly, a monster with a long neck, three humps, a pointed head, narrow slanting eyes and small pointed horns. Apparently it also shows N rolling and splashing in the water exposing a long, scaly tail. The length of this N was estimated at 9 m.

The film is alleged to be locked in a London bank vault with instructions that it cannot be released 'until such time as the public takes such matters seriously'. Since all the trustees are now dead, it is not known who owns the film and lawyers have been unable to get the film released.[126]

F3: 12 December 1933 by Malcolm Irvine. Irvine was accompanied by Stanley Clinton and Scott Hay, all of Scottish Film Productions. They were at Inverfarigaig (or on a hillside opposite Urquhart Castle) apparently with the intention of filming N. Irvine said, 'We were so excited and elated when the Monster appeared that we had no time to think of the still cameras. What you actually see on the screen lasts less than a minute, but it seemed hours when we were making it. It definitely is something with two humps – that much is clear from the picture'. He

Table 3:
List of alleged above-water cine and video films of N

No.	Date	Photographer	Location
a: cine films			
F1	c. 1935	Dr McRae	?
F2	c. 1935	Dr McRae	L Duich (?)
F3	12 Dec 1933	Malcolm Irvine	opposite Urquhart Castle
F4	15 Sep 1934	James Fraser	Uquhart Bay
F5	22 Sep 1936	Malcolm Irvine	opposite Foyers
F6	29 May 1938	G. E. Taylor	opposite Foyers
F6A	1938	James Currie	opposite Uquhart Castle
F7	23 Apr 1960	Tim Dinsdale	Foyers
F8	18 Oct 1962	LNIB	Urquhart Bay
F9	?	LNIB	?
F10	6 Jun 1963	LNIB	Urquhart Castle
F11	13 Jun 1963	LNIB	Urquhart Castle
F12	21 May 1964	Pauline Hodge	Achnahanet
F13	1 Aug 1965	Elizabeth Hall (LNIB)	Achnahanet
F14	22 May 1967	Les Durkin (LNIB)	Portclair
F15	13 Jun 1967	Dick Raynor (LNIB)	opposite Dores
F16	22 Aug 1967	Chapman/Christopher (LNIB)	?
F17	23 Aug 1967	Hunter Bros. (LNIB)	north of Invermoriston
F18	5 Oct 1967	Clem Skelton (LNIB)	opposite Foyers
F19	4 May 1968	Irvine/Young/Barnett	?
F20	27 May 1969	H. Barsky	opposite Urquhart Bay
F21	23 Jun 1969	Skelton/Davies (LNIB)	Achnahanet
F22	16 Sep 1969	Shield/Baker (LNIB)	?
F23	1966	Margaret Edward	nr. Balchraggan
F24	14 Feb 1967	Renzo Serafini	by Inverfarigaig
F25	18 Jul 1975	Alan Wilkins	Rubha Ban
F26	22 Aug 1977	Gwen Smith	Whitefield
b: video films			
V1	6 Aug 1983	John Eric Beckjord	Urquhart Bay
V2	Aug 2000	Bobbie Pollock	Invermoriston

described the object as sailing along the surface at about 4 m/s leaving a trail of foam and showing portions of its back. A description of the film in *The Times* of 4 January 1934 refers to the movement of the tail and something in the water besides the 'monster' suggesting fins or paddles. The colour was grey, with the tail nearly black. Length was estimated at nearly 5 m.

The film was shot at a range of about 100 m with a 16 mm cine camera fitted with a 75 mm lens.[127] Gould exhibited a still from the film, which shows nothing but the unknown object in the water. It cannot even be identified as having been taken on L Ness. The film was lost until 2001, when it was found and screened on television.

F4: 15 September 1934 by James Fraser (7.15 a.m.). Fraser was a member of the Mountain expedition who stayed on in the hope of seeing N. He took the film with a 16 mm cine camera fitted with a 150 mm lens in misty weather at Urquhart Bay. The range was estimated to be 1.2 km, and Kodak thought that the object was 2.4 m long. The film was shown to the 1934 annual meeting of the Linnean Society of London where two members thought that it showed a seal, one a whale, and one an otter. The film, which Burton states was 6 m long, appears to be lost. Although Mackal states that no stills were published,[128] Burton examined five published still pictures, concluding that one showed what resembled the wake of a motor-boat, that three showed wave effects caused by wind, and that one showed an anomalous object about 3.6 m long and about 100–150 m from the shore.[129]

F5: 22 September 1936 by Malcolm Irvine. Irvine claimed to have seen an unidentified object coming across the lake from Foyers. He said, 'It shows the head and neck parallel with the surface and rising and falling with the movement of the huge body. The humps are also seen rising and falling gently as the flippers move beneath them. It was over 30 ft [9 m] long and almost black in colour'.[130]

The film seems to be lost, but in 1936 it was shown to the Linnean Society, where Eric Foxon could not identify the object.[131] Whyte suspected fraud involving some mechanical device.[132] No known stills.

F6: 28 May 1938 by G. E. Taylor. This is the first colour film alleged to show N. According to Taylor, N was lying stationary opposite Foyers about 200 m from the northern shore. He stated:

> Its body was large and rounded, with a tapering to the neck which dipped under the water, becoming visible about 18 inches [45 cm] away, rising in an arch to about six inches [15 cm] above the water before dipping again. Where the arch re-entered the water it had every appearance one would associate with a head. The body showed about one foot [30 cm] above the water. Its colour was very dark.

That was at noon. Taylor drove off, but returned at 12.45 p.m. with a friend to find that the object was still in sight, but 50 m nearer. Again Taylor filmed it; now the bright sun made it look straw-coloured.[133] The film size was 16 mm.

About 1960 Burton borrowed the film for study, and exhibited a still, with an enlargement, in his 1961 book. He also produced ninety-six drawings of the object (from separate frames) and concluded that although it could be interpreted as N it was consistent with some inanimate object floating in the water. The period of the changes in the object's shape was the same as that of the waves (1.75 s). He thought that it resembled a sheet of sacking tossing on the waves, or even a vegetable mat, and that its length was about 3.6 m.[134]

Before returning the film, Burton showed it to an audience consisting of all the specialists at the then National Institute of Oceanography.[135] They were unanimous that it showed an inert body, possibly a dead horse or cow, which rose and fell in time with the waves. Burton told me that a short while before, there had been a newspaper report of a four-horned monster in the lake, which was later identified as the bloated body of a horse (with the four legs sticking upwards) and the information that a dead horse had previously been committed to a watery grave![136]

Mackal rejected Burton's conclusion and considered that the observed behaviour was compatible with fish predation. He scorned the idea that it could not be an unknown animal because it did not behave like a known one[137] (in fact it did not behave like any animal).

F6A: 1938 by James Currie. Currie, a retired London bank manager, was on holiday at L Ness where he set up a hand-turned cine camera with a 150 mm lens. For ten days he kept watch from the south shore opposite Urquhart Bay. On the eleventh day he is said to have sighted a long ripple moving at considerable speed about 275 m from the shore. He said, 'suddenly three humps broke through the water, followed by a long neck and a small triangular head. The monster was greyish-brown in colour and caused a good deal of splashing'. He claimed to have exposed between one and three minutes of film which was later processed by Kodak in London. There was no sign of interference with the film.

It is alleged that the film lies with F1 and is inaccessible for the same reason.[138]

F7: 21 April 1960 by Tim Dinsdale. On the sixth and last day of a hunt for N, Dinsdale let his car, in which he had a 16 mm Bolex cine camera mounted on a tripod, roll slowly down the road from Upper Foyers towards the Foyers Hotel. About half-way down this road he saw an object about two-thirds of the way across the lake at a range of 1189 m. Because he was not able to identify this object immediately he stopped the car and examined it through binoculars. With the naked eye he thought that the object was side-on to him, but through the binoculars it seemed to have turned away. He claims that it appeared as a long oval shape, mahogany in colour with a dark blotch on the left flank. At first it was motionless, but suddenly it began to move with visible ripples at the further end. He was convinced that he was looking at the extraordinary humped back of some huge living creature.

Dropping the binoculars, he began filming, 'firing long steady bursts of film like a machine gunner, stopping between to wind the clockwork motor'. As the object moved it seemed to change course, leaving a zig-zag wake, and then it appeared to submerge. At a point which he estimated to be two or three hundred metres from the opposite shore, it turned left and ran parallel to the shore. He was sure that only part of the creature was now above the surface, and he thought he could see successive bursts of foam from 'paddle strokes'. He estimated that the object was now 1646 m away from him.

As the object proceeded along the far shore, Dinsdale realised that there was only about 4.5 m of film left. So he stopped filming to leave a reserve in case the object ('monster') resurfaced or changed direction back towards him. His watch told him that it was four minutes since he had seen the object (at 9 a.m.), and he believed that he had exposed 6–9 m of film. In a desperate gamble he decided to get to the shore at a point west of Lower Foyers where he thought he would be nearly 915 m nearer (in fact he would be only 550 m nearer). Folding the tripod, he drove at breakneck speed down to and through Lower Foyers and onto the shore. There was nothing to be seen, not even a boat.

After breakfast he arranged with Hugh Rowand, the proprietor of the hotel, that the latter should take out a boat along the course of Dinsdale's N. This was done and Dinsdale filmed this boat, once where he had first seen the unknown object and once when it was running along the far shore. As a finale, Dinsdale paced the boat with his car and found that its maximum speed was 3.1 m/s.

Back in England, the film was developed and copied by Kodak, who projected the film in a private viewing for Dinsdale. The monochrome film disappointed Dinsdale, not only for the lack of colour but for poor contrast. He thought the film a poor imitation of what he had seen with his eyes. Plate X shows two stills from the film, which was taken through a 135 mm lens at f/11, and at a speed of 24 frames/second.

For some time Dinsdale showed the film only to friends and interested scientists, including Burton (whose camera he had used), but it was inevitable that the story would reach the press. *The Daily Mail* reported the story on 13 June 1960, and the film sequences were shown on BBC television that evening. The transfer by the BBC of the film to 35 mm and its improved contrast on a TV screen only convinced Dinsdale that he had indeed 'captured' N. Many others were also convinced, and it is this film more than anything else that stimulated the establishment of the Loch Ness (Phenomena) Investigation Bureau (LNIB) a year later. Most

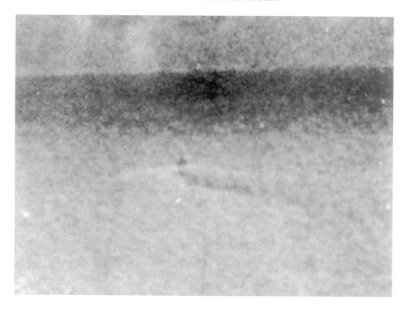

Plate X: Two stills from Dinsdale's film; top, the object Dinsdale thought was N; bottom, a boat filmed for comparison (*author's collection; copyright T. Dinsdale*).

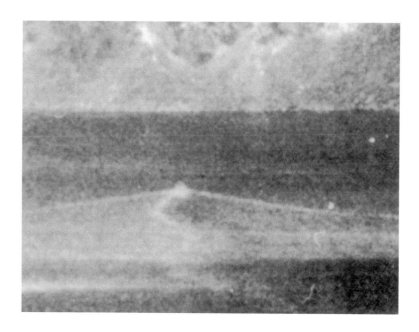

enthusiasts for N regard this film as the primary evidence for its existence, although their opinion is largely the result of subsequent analysis.[139]

F7 was analysed by JARIC at RAF Brampton, and although their original report has never been published, the LNIB reproduced its text in a leaflet.[140] JARIC argued that because the object was travelling at a speed greater than that possible for a dinghy with an outboard motor, and because a power boat, which could travel faster, would have been easily identified by means of its distinctive paintwork, it was not a surface vessel. Then, ruling out the possibility that it was a submarine, they concluded that it 'probably is [*sic*] an animate object'. Although in one paragraph they appear to argue that the object submerged, this is admitted to be a trick of the light, and their conclusion is based on the grounds of speed alone.

Although the report is generally highly regarded, it contains many defects; there are no calculations, no reference to margins of error, there is a major error in the height of the camera position (they assumed that L Ness is at sea level), and, worst of all, there is no recognition that the film is not a continuous sequence. There are also several minor errors of assumption or calculation. Although there is not space here to explain all JARIC's errors, it must be said that their principal conclusion is flawed. The speed of the unknown object was measured both as it moved away from the camera and as it moved across the field of view. The former was found to be at 4.4 m/s, while the latter (a more accurate measurement) was only 3.1 m/s. Despite this JARIC perversely concluded that the object was travelling at 4.4 m/s 'during the complete film sequence'. It can be shown that, on their assumptions and results, not only does the unknown have to make a sharp change of course (to reach their mark points), it must at some stage travel at a speed of 5.1 m/s, although they do not mention this or use it as an argument in favour of their conclusion. JARIC appear not to have realised that the camera motor only ran for some 20 s before needing to be rewound (a process that took about 12–13 s) and that Dinsdale was filming intermittently, at least in the initial sequence. In consequence, their high estimate of speed is due not to the high speed of the unknown but to their contraction of the time scale. Analysis indicates that Dinsdale filmed his N for about 90 s, only 60 s of which he recorded on film. There must have been two winding breaks, and about 8 s were lost in pauses in the initial sequence.

As a result there is no necessity for the unknown to have travelled at a speed greater than 3.1 m/s, and there is no reason to conclude that it did so. JARIC's major conclusion is therefore unfounded. The object was travelling throughout its journey at the speed of a powered dinghy. Furthermore, the results of JARIC's analysis of the shape and size of the unknown are consistent with it being a dinghy with one occupant.

Some claim (although JARIC did not) that the wake of the unknown is qualitatively different from the wake of the comparison boat. In fact it is only quantitatively different (it even shows a screw wake) and the difference is entirely due to changes in lighting and the surface conditions.

Relevant to interpretation of F7 is the fact that only two months later, Burton and his party observed powered dinghies travelling almost the same route as Dinsdale's N; they even saw them appear to vanish just as Dinsdale had done.[27] Later Burton discovered that a local farmer was in the habit of taking a dinghy across at the very time that Dinsdale was filming N.[141]

F8: 17 October 1962 by the LNIB.[142] During the LNIB's first expedition, seven members saw and filmed a 'long dark shape' moving through the water of Urquhart Bay during the afternoon. The object, which was about 200 m away, 'visibly disturbed the fish'. Although JARIC determined that it was not a wave effect,[143] Mackal found it unconvincing.[144]

F10: 6 June 1963 by the LNIB. A 16 mm film sequence of a large object at just over 3.2 km range (!) moving through shallow water and eventually remaining stationary. No conclusions were reached.[145]

F11: 13 June 1963 by the LNIB. This film shows an object which was bobbing up and down about 1 km away, but a heavy heat haze makes it unclear.[146]

F12: May 1964 by Pauline Hodge. Peter Hodge and his wife Pauline were camping on the field at Achnahanet previously used by the LNIB. Peter noticed a pole-like object sticking out of the water just above the tree line, but when he slammed a car door it disappeared. A second later a wash was seen heading away across the water. No stills have been published, but Mackal states that all it shows is a wash at too great a range to merit analysis.[147]

F14: 22 May 1967 by Les Durkin of the LNIB. This is a 15 s film of waves or humps moving against the wind. JARIC concluded that the range was 915 m and that the disturbed areas were 11–15 m long, 0.6 m high, and moving at approximately 3 m/s. They could not see humps specifically or any solid object.[148] No stills have been published, but Mackal states that the phenomena are 'clearly identifiable as waves'; probably caused by a vessel which was known to be in the area'.[149]

F15: 13 June 1967 by Dick Raynor of the LNIB. Raynor filmed a disturbance near Dores at a range of about 1.5 km on a flat calm surface, and the film includes a view of *Scot II*, which was passing at the time. JARIC identified the disturbance as a wash or wake pattern converging on the far shore at about 2.2 m/s, but Mackal, who published three stills, considered that it qualified as an authentic film of a large animal in L Ness and that it corroborates F7.[150]

F17: 23 August 1967 by Christopher S. and Jeffrey W. Hunter of the LNIB. A film in calm but hazy conditions of something repeatedly diving. Although JARIC thought it unlikely to be a bird, Mackal, who viewed the film carefully, concluded that this was the explanation.[151]

F25: 18 July 1975 by Alan Wilkins. An unclear film taken with a 16 mm camera fitted with a 300 mm lens from a caravan site at Rubha Ban. No stills published, but see account under P18.

F26: 22 August 1977 by Gwen Smith. Peter and Gwen Smith were standing on the shore almost opposite Urquhart Castle, with the weather worsening and becoming cloudy after a fairly calm day. At about 5.05 p.m. an object emerged, rising vertically from the water about 160 m away to the left. Through binoculars Peter saw that it was a 'strangely thick' periscope-like object. It had a thick, rectangular head with no visible features on a powerful long neck at least 30 cm thick. It was leathery-brown in colour and at one point appeared to be the height of a man.

Plate XI: A still from Gwen Smith's film of N (*Fortean Picture Library; copyright Gwen Smith*).

As it started to sink, Gwen filmed it with an 8 mm Printz T3 Zoom camera loaded with colour film. The object surfaced three more times and Gwen filmed two of these events. During either the second or third appearance the object was seen to turn its head either directly away from or directly towards the Smiths, reflecting the sunlight which was just breaking through over Urquhart Castle. The object finally disappeared at 5.15 p.m. (see Plate XI).

Dinsdale also acquired a report on the same incident from Christopher Idle, a schoolboy from Yorkshire who claimed to be collecting data for a school project with a friend (John Coulton). They had a long line with various hooks and bait going out into the water, but it was weighted with a large stone. As Christopher was out in their boat John saw something surface and dive several times. He told Christopher on his return and they both spoke to the Smiths. After rowing back along the shore, and as he turned the boat towards the shore, a 'large black THING' poked up a metre or so out of the water, so close to the boat that he could have hit it with an oar. He described the neck as tapering from about 45 cm wide at the surface to 22 cm where it joined the head, which was like that of a sheep, but larger. There was no obvious demarcation between neck and head and he saw no other features. He could not even say, from his brief sighting, that it was alive. The object rose vertically, paused, and then sank with head dipping forward. He was sure that it was not a log, otter, deer, or a mass of rotting vegetation.

Since it has been suggested that Idle and Coulton were responsible for a hoax, it is worth noting the Smiths' opinion of them. They thought that the boys were genuine, straightforward, good-humoured, and interested and bemused by the event. They thought that Idle in particular was somewhat shaken and that this explained his excessive jocularity. Neither withheld any personal information and Idle submitted a report to Dinsdale. Their only visible apparatus was the fishing line, which was attached to a small drum on the shore. The Smiths were sure that they would have seen any manipulation of cords to operate a submerged model. At the time of the fourth sighting, Coulton was clearly visible on the shore while Idle was rowing ashore. Peter Smith offered many other reasons for rejecting the hoax hypothesis.

In 1978 JARIC issued a one-page report on their examination of the film. They concluded that the object was between 157 and 168 m from the camera and that it had a fairly uniform width of 20 cm (conflicting with Idle's description). Its maximum height was 76 cm and it moved sideways a distance of only 60 cm. JARIC attempted densitometer traces across the object, resulting in the conclusion that it was 'roughly rectangular'. However, they admitted that this profile cannot be relied on with such a poor image. They noted that the object rose and fell three

times during the sequence, independent of the wave motion, and that
this pointed to much more of the object lying under the water (this is not
the only explanation).[152]
The Loch Ness and Morar Project have demonstrated how an
inanimate object, perhaps a timber post, could have been manipulated
with a single line. Idle's school knew nothing about a project and he has
not responded to my enquiries.

Video Film

V1: 6 August 1983 by John Erik Beckjord. The operator is an American
wildlife photographer who came to L Ness representing the National
Cryptozoological Society.[153] He set up two video cameras, one at
the Clansman Hotel and one in the old croft buildings at St Ninians
overlooking the western corner of Urquhart Bay. The cameras were
fitted with telephoto or zoom lenses and polarised filters, and they were
adapted to operate in a stop-frame mode enabling the tape to run for
100 hours. Beckjord claimed that on the above date the camera at St
Ninians caught N, but it was hard to make out anything in the picture. It
is alleged that the object in the picture is some 200 m out from the shore,
but Hepple, who watched the Bay for four hours that day (during which
time the incident is alleged to have occurred), saw nothing unusual.
The N sequence shows an object and several wakes moving over
about 100 m of water in Urquhart Bay. Then it appears that two objects
dive in different directions causing two large splashes which show as a
v-shape. One leg of the splash is 21 m long. After the splash subsides
there appear to be three dark, wide objects swimming off at an angle to
the splash in the direction of the Castle. Beckjord speculated that there
were three large N underwater and that they caused wakes when they
occasionally surfaced. He was convinced that the wakes could not have
been caused by water birds, but Hepple is sure that waterfowl, which he
saw that day, were responsible, probably as they took off. Beckjord has
not stated the speed of the objects. Hepple notes that the stills provided
of the moment of the splash (see Plate XII) show no evidence of waves
and he doubts that at the low angle of photography anything could be
seen underwater.[154]

V2: August 2000 by Bobbie Pollock. Only in March 2002, did Pollock, a
Glasgow postman, reveal that he had taken a 32 min. video of an object
in Invermoriston Bay two years earlier. Apparently he 'feared ridicule'.
In fact he won £500 from bookmaker William Hill for the best recent
'Nessie sighting' on the recommendation of the Official Loch Ness
Monster Fan Club which administers the annual award. He and his wife

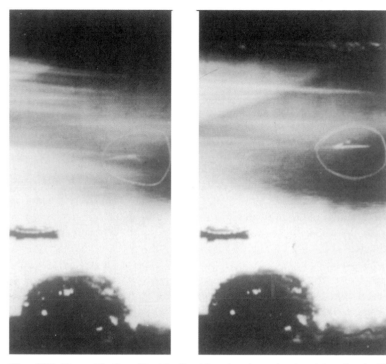

Plate XII: Two stills from Beckjord's video showing what he claimed to be N (location rings added) (*author's collection; copyright J. E. Beckjord*).

and child were resting at the stone seat overlooking the Bay when they saw a floating object which started moving off towards Fort Augustus (southwards) 'at quite a pace' and which rose 1.5 m out of the water. He claimed that the object was neither a seal nor a deer. The video sequence, which was shown on Scottish television, was studied by Mark Stewart, curator of marine mammals at the Scottish Sea Life Sanctuary in Oban. Stewart felt that, although the object sometimes looked like a seal, it was moving too quickly. Due to unsteady filming, the image shown on TV moves about too much for any conclusion to be drawn. As a result of the video, bookmakers cut the odds on N's existence from 500-1 to 250-1.[154A]

5

The Underwater
Photographic Evidence

So far the only underwater photographs alleged to show N are those taken by Robert Rines and his associates from the Academy of Applied Science. Table 4 lists the photographs, which will be discussed below. The principal account of the taking of these photographs (and the accompanying sonar record, which is dealt with in the next chapter) is contained in an article which Rines, Wyckoff, Edgerton, and Klein wrote in 1976.[155]

Table 4:
List of the AAS photographs of N

No.	Date	Location	Popular Title
U1	8 Aug 1972	Urquhart Bay	'flipper'
U2	8 Aug 1972	Urquhart Bay	'flipper' *
U3	8 Aug 1972	Urquhart Bay	'two body'
U4	20 Jun 1975	Urquhart Bay	'upper torso, neck and head'
U5	20 Jun 1975	Urquhart Bay	'gargoyle head'

Note:
U1/2/3 are referred to by Mackal as P16, and U4/5 as P17.
AAS: Academy of Applied Science.

U1/2/3: 8 August 1972. On the night of 7/8 August 1972, Rines, assisted by some members of the LNIB, deployed two boats in Urquhart Bay not far from Temple Pier. One boat (*Narwhal*) carried sonar equipment which that night detected targets alleged to have been N. It is alleged that the sonar targets were identical with the objects photographed by the underwater camera suspended from the other boat (*Nan*). The boats were about 36 m apart, *Nan* further from the shore than *Narwhal*, with the camera equipment dropped onto an 'underwater ridge' in about 13 m of water. Rines claimed that both the sonar transducer and the camera were on this ridge, 'aimed across a deep underwater valley'. It is alleged that the camera was so aimed that an object in the sonar beam would also be in the camera's range.

The camera-strobe system was one developed and built by Professor Harold Edgerton at MIT. It consisted of a 16 mm time-lapse motion picture camera and a 50 Ws strobe light, each housed in its own cylindrical case. The camera had a fixed focal length of 10 mm and an aperture of f/1.8. It was synchronized with an electronic flash unit and an adjustable timer set to take pictures at 45 s intervals. The exposure time of the camera was 10 ms and the flash duration was 1 ms. The film was Kodachrome II with an ISO speed of 25.

It was thought that the camera may have photographed the targets detected by the sonar, and the film was rushed for development the next day. It was found that out of 2000 frames exposed only three showed anything. Two adjacent frames, and another taken three minutes later, showed vague and unclear objects (see Plate XIII). It has not been stated at what precise time these photographs were taken or what relative position the 'object' frames occupied in the whole film reel.

To clarify the indistinct pictures, they were enhanced by digital signal processing at JPL. This work was done by Alan Gillespie, then a graduate student in geology working as a junior engineer. JPL allowed him to use one of their computers in his own time. To enhance the photographs, he adopted conventional techniques similar to those used

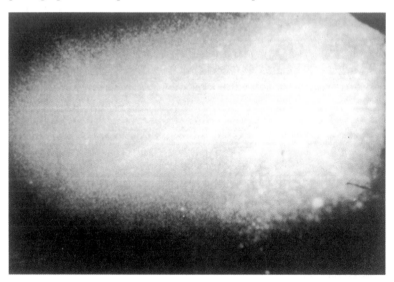

Plate XIII: The original (unenhanced) photograph of U2; the originals of U1 and U3 are similar (*author's collection; copyright Academy of Applied Science*).

to enhance satellite photographs. The pictures were scanned by electronic equipment which divided each one into two million pixels and assigned numbers to these on the basis of brightness. The numbers were stored on magnetic tape, fed through a computer and then recombined to form an image in which the original contrast was exaggerated and the detail more sharply defined.[156]

The result of the enhancement process is in some doubt. According to Rines, the result was the appearance (in U1 and U2) of clearly defined diamond-shaped objects which appear to be attached to a larger body (see Plate XIV). Not only that, but the object is clearly in a different position on the two adjacent frames, indicating movement. (U3 is unclear but is alleged to show 'two bodies'.) Because the diamond shape, which is taken to be a limb of N, is in focus it is claimed that it must be at least 1.2 m from the camera and so between 1.2 and 2 m long.[157] If true this would certainly be evidence for the existence of a very large N, although there are anatomical objections to the shape of the 'flipper'. Dinsdale exhibited a picture of the most complete skeleton known of a long-necked plesiosaurus, from which it is evident that its limbs were not rhomboid.

In September 1984 it was alleged that the pictures published by Rines were not those produced by Gillespie's enhancement process and that Rines had retouched the pictures to show a clear 'flipper'. A copy of the enhanced but unretouched picture was obtained from Gillespie and compared with Rines's published version.[158] This brought a response from Wyckoff, who denied the allegations. He claimed that the published pictures were composites combining several different computer-enhanced digital reconstructions, but admitted that they ought to have been captioned 'composite photographs of successive original film transparancies using several different JPL computer-enhanced digital reconstructions from the original film transparancies'! He suggested that some retouching may have been done by various newspapers and magazines who had published the photographs, although there was no admission that this was done by *Technology Review*, who published a picture identical to those which appear to have been retouched.[159]

Many suggestions have been made as to the identity of the rhomboid object. Some think that it is the fin of a large fish or eel. Halstead *et al.* believed that it is the steering rudder of a Viking ship (an idea related to interpretation of U5 as the dragon-headed prow of the same ship).[160] There is no independent archaeological evidence for this idea and there has been no expedition to lift such a valuable artefact. Scott rightly demolished the Viking ship argument.[161]

The camera geometry and picture analysis show that to be in focus the objects in the pictures must be at least 82 cm from the camera, and,

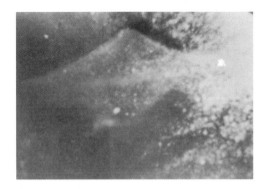

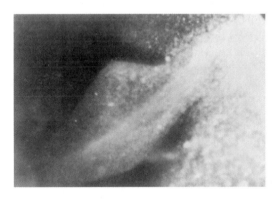

Plate XIV: The result of enhancement of U1 (top), U2 (centre), and U3 (bottom) according to the Academy of Applied Science (*author's collection; copyright claimed by the Academy of Applied Science, but the pictures are allegedly the product of JPL*).

therefore, that they are at least 50 cm long. As Mackal has observed, even this is much more substantial than the pectoral fins of the largest possible fish known in L Ness.[162]

In response to a request for copies of both enhanced and unenhanced versions of U1/2 Rines sent me two slides. The one marked 'unenhanced' is reproduced as Plate XIII and agrees with all published versions of that picture. The one marked 'enhanced' is shown as Plate XV and differs considerably from Plate XIV. This difference tends to confirm the allegations made by Razdan and Kielar. When I asked Rines (in July 1984) why there was this marked difference he expressed the view that there were much better reproductions in his office. By 'better' he must have meant that they show more clearly the rhomboid 'flipper', and we now understand from Wyckoff that these pictures have been produced by an accumulation process. Sir Frank Claringbull of the British Museum is reported as saying that the pictures (he may have been referring to both the 1972 and 1975 pictures) are of 'a piece of tree' and that an 'element of hoax could not be excluded'.[163]

U4/5: 20 July 1975. On the night of 19/20 June 1975, Rines, again assisted by LNIB personnel, deployed sonar and cameras suspended from boats (*Hunter*, plus tender) in an area south-east of Temple Pier not far from the shore, where he claimed that the water depth was about

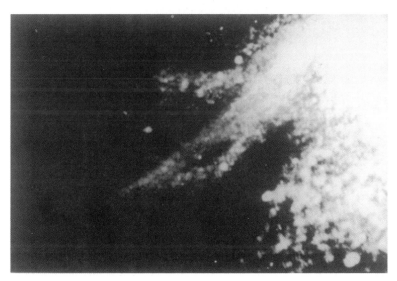

Plate XV: The enhanced version of U2 sent to the author by R. H. Rines (*author's collection; copyright as for Plate XIV*).

25 m. The main array consisted of sonar transducer, camera, and strobe light, with the camera and strobe linked to the sonar in such a way that it only took a picture if the sonar detected an object with a cross-section of not less than 1.2–1.5 m at a distance of less than 12 m. This array was set on the bottom aimed upwards at an angle of about 45°.

As a back-up system the 1972 apparatus was suspended in mid-water (12 m) but with camera and strobe now separated by 1.5 m vertically, with the camera below the strobe. The strobe was aimed horizontally and the camera was aimed upwards at an angle of about 45°. The system was set to take pictures regularly at 1.2 minute intervals. Film was Ektachrome with an ISO speed of 125.

In the event the main array became covered with silt and produced no results (except that the sonar recorded some targets, which may have been the back-up array). However, pictures were taken by the back-up system, as shown in Table 5.

Table 5:
List of the AAS photographs taken in 1975

AAS ref.	My ref.	Date	Time (BST)	Description
A		19 June	0945	unknown
B		19 June	2230	cylindrical object
C	U4	20 June	0432	'upper torso, neck and head'
D		20 June	0540	unidentified object preceded by a view of underside of the boat
E	U5	20 June	1145	'head' preceded and followed by view of underside of the boat
F		20 June	1650	unidentified silhouette after agitation of the camera

The object in picture A is unclear, but picture B evidently shows part of the bottom, although Rines thinks that it must be a roughly cylindrical object such as a branch in midwater. Picture C is famous for being interpreted to show what appears to be the upper torso, neck and head of a living creature (see Plate XVI), although there are no consecutive pictures showing it in a different position. Picture D was more easily interpreted as a branch or a tree trunk, and picture F could have the same cause. Picture E is interpreted by Rines to show the head of a creature (N?) with bilateral symmetry in half profile, with the nostrils and open mouth at the right, and several horn-like projections at the top.

Because pictures D and E are adjacent to frames which show views

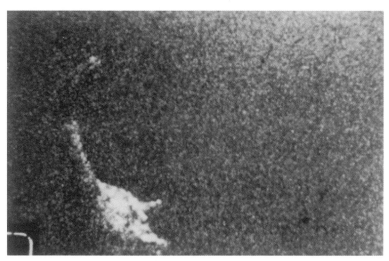

Plate XVI: The picture (U4) which the Academy of Applied Science claims shows N's upper torso, neck and head (*author's collection; copyright Academy of Applied Science*).

of the underside of the support boat, it was assumed by Rines that N disturbed the suspended array, intermittently getting its photograph taken. It is rumoured that the pictures have been computer-enhanced, but enhanced pictures have not been published.

Rines claims that the distance, and hence the size, of the objects in the picture can be determined from light densitometer measurements and he exhibited a plot of image density against the log relative exposure (light reflected from objects) for 'high-speed ektachrome [*sic*] film'. Kodak Ltd, the manufacturer of Ektachrome, to whom I showed this graph, denied that they had produced it. From this plot Rines determined that the 'torso' in U4 was about 7.5 m from the camera and that the 'head' was only 4.5 m away. He estimated that the visible 'body' was at least 5.4 m long, and that the 'torso' was about 2 m across. Similarly, he determined that the object in U5 was about 1.5 m from the camera and that it was about 60 cm long. His calculations seem to have made no allowance for foreshortening due to refraction at the air/water interface of the camera housing.

While it is possible to determine the distance of an object from a camera by measuring its image density, this can only be accomplished if the reflectance of the object is known. The graph exhibited by Rines is for an 18 per cent grey card, the reflectance of which is known (18 per cent). But no one knows the reflectance of N, or the reflectance of the objects in U4 and U5 if they are not N. A further complication is the turbidity of the water, which would alter the plot of density against reflected light. It is possible to calibrate the distance of a known object in L Ness, but it is not possible to calibrate an unknown.

Harwood, discussing the 1975 pictures, concluded that the image sharpness tells us little about the object's distance from the camera, except that if it is out of focus it was very close indeed to the lens.[164] However, he made distance assessments based on the angle at which the light strikes the objects and the resultant modelling. Based on comparison photographs, he concluded that in U4 the flash to subject distance was comparable to the flash to camera distance (about 1.5 m). A subject distance of 2 m would give a 'body' length of 480 mm (not allowing for refraction), which Harwood compared with the size and shape of the horned head of a Highland cow. Similar arguments led Harwood to conclude that the object in U5 is only about 375 mm across, even though he agreed with Rines that it was 1.5 m away.[165] He noted its resemblance to a cloud of silt, a photograph of which he exhibited.[166] His conclusions imply that the camera photographed debris and silt on the bottom of L Ness.

Early in 1976, Dick Raynor, who assisted Rines in both 1972 and 1975, had occasion to advise divers in Urquhart Bay. After mooring to a buoy off Temple Pier they found that it was secured to Rines's 1975 array, part of the steelwork of which was protruding from the silt. However, they discovered that, according to their depth gauges, the depth was not 25 m but 18 m. This prompted Raynor to take a boat out to the buoy in order to investigate. He found that if he pulled in all the slack on the buoy's mooring rope (2.4 m) the depth under the boat directly over the array was about 15 m. He reckoned that there was about 3 m of slack in the rope and that this would allow the buoy to move over a circle of radius 11 m (taking the depth as 18 m). In fact, if *Hunter* was moored with 5 m of rope to the buoy, it could put the backup array 16 m from the primary array. Raynor found that with such a mooring, and a force 3 wind from the south-west, there was only 10 m of water under the boat. Moored within 0.6 m of the buoy, there was 12 m. He concluded that an onshore wind could easily have put the back-up array into water shallower than its suspension depth of 12 m, and that it would have begun to roll on the bottom, such rolling being facilitated by its triangular shape.[167]

If the back-up array touched and possibly rolled on the bottom then the photographs obtained by it are most likely to be of bottom debris, and Harwood's explanation of U4/5 becomes realistic. Indeed, U5 makes more sense if one assumes that the array was lying on its side on the bottom. By turning the picture through 90° (see Plate XVII) we see a picture of bottom debris illuminated by the the strobe to the left.[168] It may be that U4 ought also to be turned. This hypothesis also explains

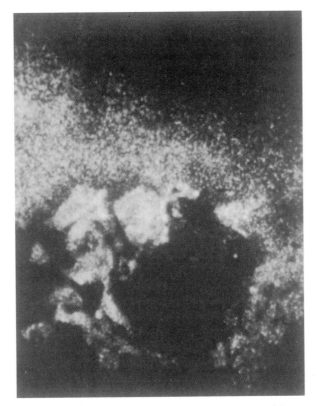

Plate XVII: The picture (U5) which the Academy of Applied Science claims shows N's 'grotesque' head (turn page 90° clockwise). In this orientation it shows bottom debris (*author's collection, copyright Academy of Applied Science*).

the pictures of the surface showing the boat; the array was lying on its back on the bottom. The possibility that the camera touched bottom and so tilted up or down was suggested by Shine in 1980.[169] It is now known that the object in U5 is a tree stump; the stump has been recovered.

An attempt by the AAS to repeat their 1972 and 1975 results, using a battery of different cameras, brought a negative result.

6

The Sonar and Radar Evidence

While water is a poor transmitter of light, or any electromagnetic radiation, it readily transmits sound. Sound waves travel much faster through solids and liquids than through air, and they can be detected at much greater distances. Indeed, it is by means of sound that seismometers detect underground nuclear tests or earthquakes on the other side of the Earth.

A sonar system consists essentially of two components. One is the control equipment, including the sound generator and a means of visualising the result either in the form of a chart on which a pen records reflected sounds or on a CRO. The other component is the transducer, a sort of loudspeaker which is placed underwater and which both generates and receives the sound impulses. The transducer is designed to throw the sound beam in one direction (which may be variable) and the angle at which the beam spreads can also be controlled. This beam width is defined in angular width of beam between those points where the intensity of sound is one half of that on the main axis of the transducer (i.e. at the 3 dB points). Sound may therefore be emitted at angles greater than those specified for a particular transducer, and these sound pulses are usually called 'side lobes'.

Acoustic resolution is very much inferior to visual resolution by reason of the very much greater wavelength. Consequently sonar cannot tell the size (without other information) or shape of an object. However it compensates by being able to give accurate information on distance and bearing of the target, provided certain precautions are taken. The sound is emitted in pulses about 1 ms long at a rate of between 5 and 1000 per minute.

If some object which has acoustic properties different from those of water lies in the sound's path, some of the pulse energy is reflected and spreads out from the object as if it were a sound source. Some of this energy reaches the transducer and is detected and recorded. The strength of the echo will be a function of the degree to which the density of the object differs from that of water, the size of the object, and its range. Since the range is determined via the same equipment the only two parameters that can mingle are density and size. The flesh of fish differs very little in density from that of water and so gives a weak sonar signal. In fish more than half the signal comes from the gas-filled swim bladder, which is relatively small. (Being filled with gas the bladder has a density very different from water.) An aquatic animal with lungs gives a much stronger signal, but then so do other objects. In order to resolve the question of whether or not a particular target was N, Baker and Westwood set three criteria:

(1) the density of the echo
(2) evidence of movement, especially rapid movement
(3) change of depth and objects at unusual depths, i.e. below the normal fish levels.

They noted that none of these criteria was foolproof; a very strong echo could indicate a submerged log, a densely packed fish shoal, or even some other very large animal such as a huge eel. Movement could be given by fish, although fish do not suddenly change depth. Objects at great depth could be eels or salmon kelts, or even a dense shoal of char.[170]

In short, positive identification of a sonar target is only possible if the target has been observed previously by sonar and there is a high degree of correlation between the two sets of observations. In the case of N, no such database exists and classification is impossible.[171]

Sonar cannot locate targets that are close to other powerful reflectors of sound, such as the bottom and walls of L Ness and its surface. In particular it cannot detect a target that is close inshore. It is thought that these limitations explain the failure to detect eels or otters.

If an object moves relative to a sonar beam, this movement will be detected. On a pen-graph recorder, the paper feeds continuously past the oscillating pen, and the graph shows time increasing in the direction opposite to the direction of its travel. The other ordinate of the graph shows distance from the transducer. An object passing transversely across the sonar beam will produce a crescent shape as its echo is plotted. This is because the sound vector shortens as the object approaches the centre of the beam and lengthens as it heads again for the edge of the beam. However, the same result could be obtained with a stationary target and a moving transducer, or even a target which drifts gradually towards and then away from the transducer. In all cases where the chart shows relative movement it is vital to know whether or not the transducer itself was moving.

A change in range shows on the chart as a diagonal line, the gradient of the line being steeper with faster changes of range. Constant range shows as a line parallel to the side of the chart. Generally sonar systems cannot tell the operator where (apart from the range) a target is in the beam; it cannot point out a particular direction. Consequently a sonar gives only one component (that in line with the transducer) of a moving target's velocity vector; it cannot tell in which direction the target is moving.

Sonars may be 'active' or 'passive'. Active sonar is that which both emits and receives a sound pulse. Passive sonar is that which only receives a sound pulse, in effect a directional hydrophone. Creasey argues that because there is little or no evidence that N makes much noise, and because if it does there are no data which could be used for classification, the use of passive sonar in L Ness is ineffective. Although an array of hydrophones could be used to obtain directional information, range would have to be obtained via a number of separate passive sonars. Passive sonar has the advantage that it creates no noise, unlike active systems which, although they operate at frequencies inaudible to known acquatic animals, can create audible sound through an unbalanced transmitter or too high a signal level.[172]

There are four main types of active sonar, as follows:

Echo-sounder

A system usually used to find (sound) depth of water or depth of fish shoals. The array points vertically downwards beneath the hull of the vessel on which it is mounted. To allow for ship roll and pitching movements, the array beam-width is usually quite large.

Searchlight sonar

A system where the array is rotated and tilted to obtain the angular coordinate of the target. If the rotation of the array is used for search purposes, then if a high resolution is required the resulting data rate is too low to allow trace to trace correlation on the display. It is the trace to trace correlation which enables a moving target to be detected against a stationary background.

Sidescan sonar

Sidescan sonar has a fan-shaped beam typically 0.5° horizontally by 20° vertically. In its usual mode of operation the array is fixed either on the hull of a vessel or in a small hydrodynamically-stable towed body. The beam is aimed at right angles to the direction of travel but tilted downwards. This produces echoes from the bottom which are plotted on a chart recorder as a map of the bed. Mid-water targets become plotted on the chart at the appropriate slant range and their true nature is concealed. Sidescan sonars can be mounted stationary in the water when they give a display of range against time; any target within the sonar beam which changes range will show as a slanting line on the chart.

Multiple beam-forming sonar

The major disadvantage of the searchlight sonar is the low data rate caused by the relatively slow speed of sound. The data rate may be increased considerably by forming not a single search beam but a number of separate beams which will cover the whole of the desired scanned sector. These beams are formed electronically. The result is that in a system which forms n-beams simultaneously the data rate is increased n-times. The array has to be stabilised against roll, pitch and yaw.

Various lists of sonar operations in L Ness have been produced,[173] but they do not all agree. Here I attempt a reconciliation based on Creasey's list of searchers but restricted to those who claimed contact with N, or whose unknown contacts have been identified with N by others (see Table 6). The following pages describe each sonar operation or the circumstances in which a contact was obtained. More is known about some operations than others.

S1: 3 December 1954; Rival III. On this date the Peterhead drifter *Rival III* passed southwards through L Ness on her way down the Caledonian Canal to the West Coast fishing grounds. Mate Peter Anderson was at the wheel.

It is reported that as the boat neared Urquhart Castle N was detected by the echo-sounder (since commercial fishing is forbidden in L Ness there was no reason for the echo-sounder to be operating). The skipper and other members of the crew were taking their mid-morning break in the cabin below. A newspaper reported as follows:

> Suddenly, he [Anderson] stiffened . . . The graph needle had started to chart an astonishing image. And for three minutes . . . he watched the outline of the 'monster' taking shape under the drifter's keel 90 fathoms [165 m] below.
>
> His calculations showed the object was 50 feet [15 m] long and lying in the centre of two large rock shelves. 'I've laughed at people talking about monsters in the loch . . . but I've never seen anything and I've been through it dozens of times. There I was, standing quite casually, when suddenly the printer arm in the machine started to draw this thing on the roll of recording paper. As it sketched it out I couldn't believe my eyes. For several minutes the arm went on moving and the outlines of the thing below the water were drawn on the paper. I shouted to the crew and they came crowding up to the wheelhouse. They were amazed, as I was. At once we turned the boat about and tried to trace the 'monster' again. But it was no use. We thought we had frightened it away.[174]

A photograph of the chart from the recorder with the alleged image of N is shown in Plate XVIII. The echo-sounder in question was made by Kelvin Hughes and the newspaper claimed that the company's technical

Table 6:
List of alleged* sonar contacts with N

No.	Date	Sonar operator	Location	Type of sonar
S1	3 Dec 1954	Fishing boat *Rival III*	north basin	echo sounder
S2	15 May 1958	BBC's puffer *Kaffir*	Urquhart Bay	echo sounder
S3	Dec 1959	Fishing boat *Guiding Star*	off Foyers	echo sounder
S4	27 Jun 1960+	Arnold/Baker (Oxford & Cambridge Unis)	?	searchlight
S5	1962	Baker/Westwood (Cambridge Uni.)	various	echo sounders
S6	28 Aug 1968	University of Birmingham	Urquhart Bay	multibeam
S7	1969	Vickers Oceanics Ltd	Urquhart Bay	searchlight
S8	10 Oct 1969	Robert E Love	2 km NE of Foyers	searchlight
S9	22 Oct 1970	Jeffrey Blonder	nr. Invermoriston	?
S10	1970	Rines/Klein	Urquhart Bay and elsewhere	sidescan
S11	8 Aug 1972	Rines/LNIB	Urquhart Bay	echo sounder
S12	30 June 1976	Klein Associates/AAS	Urquhart Bay	sidescan
S13	1 Jul 1976	Klein Associates/AAS	Urquhart Bay	sidescan
S14	1975	Partech Electronics	?	?
S15	1978	Theo Brown	0.6 km SW of Foyers	?
S16	Apr 1981	Fishing boat *Provider II*	north basin	echo sounder
S17	1981	Loch Ness & Morar Project	various	echo sounder
S18	1982	Loch Ness & Morar Project	various	searchlight
S19	July 1992	Project Urquhart	by Invermoriston	sidescan

Notes:

Numbering differs from that of Mackal.

+ expedition period was from this date until 23 July 1960.

* if not alleged by the operator, alleged by others.

List does not include some other contacts mentioned by Witchell (March 1964, *Girl Norma*; April 1969, *Ha-Burn*; April 1970, *Tea Rose*) due to lack of details.

expert, L. A. Southcott, had examined the chart with a magnifying glass. He was quoted as saying:

> The paper and ink are definitely genuine, I can certify that it hasn't been tampered with in any way. It is a true impression on [*sic*] an object. From the calibrated scale on the graph it is 50 ft [15 m] long. The vessel has passed right over the object and the machine has held it on the graph for three minutes to get that fine impression. This is definitely animal matter of some kind. This is proved by the fact that echoes from the sounding

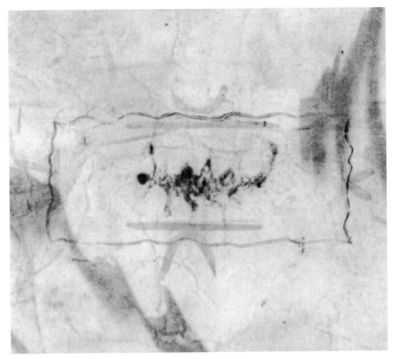

Plate XVIII: Part of the echo-sounder chart from *Rival III*; the box and arrows have been added (*IPC Newspapers Ltd, who hold copyright in the picture, but not in the chart*).

machine have passed right through the object onto the loch-bed below. The graph tells us this object cannot be solid rock or even wreckage. It is floating about 30 fathoms [55 m] from the loch bed. In all my experience I've never seen anything like this. This object certainly isn't a whale or like any other kind of fish that has been charted. This is truly amazing.[175]

The following day's issue of the same newspaper, which had obtained exclusive rights to the story, reported that the chart had been taken back to Kelvin Hughes in Glasgow for close scrutiny. There it was examined by Arthur Sutton from Eastbourne; he was described as a 54-year-old expert on echo-sounder equipment for the fishing industry and head of Kelvin Hughes's technical department in Scotland. He is reported to have said:

If this were a large animal in the loch, this is the kind of image an echo-sounder would give. It is definitely not a water-logged tree or a shoal of fish. These give entirely different signals. The object has been struck by 380 pings from the machine.[176]

Eleven days later the newspaper published a scientific summary by Maurice Burton after he had discussed the evidence with Donald Gow, another Kelvin Hughes expert. Gow, an authority on echo-sounders, made three observations:

1. An echo-sounding machine tells only of the existence of solid matter in the water; it is not designed to define shapes or even sizes. An operator can tell what certain familiar objects are – such as shoals of fish – because they repeat more or less the same pattern.

2. A solid object is likely to give a 'reflected echo' – which probably means that all the marks below the main body are merely reflections of the upper marks, which themselves are probably elongated.

3. The large blotch which might be interpreted as the head is certainly the usual mark made by the pen of the graph when it 'signs off'.

Burton thought that the evidence pointed to the creature being a giant eel. [177]

Further investigation shows that no confidence can be placed in the opinions of Southcott and Sutton. When interpreted in the light of the data provided by the manual for the echo-sounder in question (Kelvin Hughes MS24A), the chart reveals that the object was apparently recorded for about 6 min., not 3. Furthermore, if the object was stationary, and only 15 m long, then the boat's speed was only 2.6 m/min! From the bottom profiles, and taking them as profiles of the bottom of L Ness, it can be shown that the speed of the boat was about 2.8 m/s. In that case, if the object was stationary it was over 1 km long. The object is not lying between two large rock shelves; the peaks on either side of the object are records of the bottom in two different depth phases, one shifted 109 m relative to the other.

Although Southcott assured Whyte that the chart could not be faked in any way,[178] there was a way in which it could be done. The recorder was fitted with an 'electric' pencil. This was a stylus that could be hand operated to write on the chart. If someone had used it to draw the picture of N, the resultant stain would have been identical to that of the normal stylus (although it would not show the sweep marks). It can be seen that there is a different quality about the mark for N on the chart. It is even possible to make such a drawing on the chart before rewinding it back into the recorder, so playing a practical joke on the operator, who could not tell that the object was not real. It is reported that Anderson has admitted to staff at the Loch Ness Centre that the whole thing was a hoax, but one in which Kelvin Hughes conspired.

S2: 15 May 1958; BBC. On the 25th anniversary of the phenomenon the BBC broadcast a live TV programme from L Ness. The programme included the use of a Marconi echo-sounder. Although this equipment detected nothing unusual during the broadcast, it is reported that about an hour beforehand an object was detected 70 m north-east of Urquhart Castle. It appeared to dive away from the vessel between 5 and 18 m deep 'causing considerable agitation', and the operator thought that it was about 6 m long. None of the Marconi technicians could identify it.[179]

S3: 5 December 1959; Guiding Star. Near Foyers this fishing vessel's echo-sounder found a target at a depth of 173 m, which is very near to the bottom depth opposite Foyers itself. The newspaper illustration of the chart is unclear (showing a rising profile followed by a break in the record). It was examined by the manufacturer (unknown) who stated that the recording differed in no way from that obtained from a fish shoal.[180] In 1960 Baker and Arnold reported the discovery of what appeared to be salmon kelts at a depth of 150 m or so;[181] 173 m on a saltwater recorder is equivalent to about 155 m in fresh water.

S4: 27 June to 23 July 1960; Oxford and Cambridge Universities. Stimulated by a lecture given by Dr Denys Tucker, more than thirty graduates and undergraduates organised an expedition to L Ness. They deployed a Marconi Marine searchlight sonar which ranged over a hemisphere of water 400 m in radius (deeper than L Ness). Once detected, a target was followed, and the results were plotted on a chart recorder.

'Crescent' recordings were obtained from fish greater than 90 cm long (or from drifting inanimate objects) at different depths down to 36 m. In addition some objects appeared to be diving. On one occasion, with the sonar in the vertical position, the diving trace appeared to connect to a 'crescent' trace. The dive was by something 'dense' (i.e. it produced a strong signal) which moved from the surface to 18 m depth at a speed calculated to be at least 1.8 m/s (the published chart shows an object to have reached a depth of 47 m, indicating a dive of nearly one minute duration). Almost immediately the object climbed back up and contact was lost. A little later, a similar object produced a 'crescent' (shown on their chart as a diagonal crescent and indicating a dive transverse to the sonar beam). The expedition could not identify this diving object.[182]

S5: 1962; Cambridge University. The Cambridge component of the 1960 expedition arranged another expedition in 1962. It was decided to sweep the lake from end to end using a fleet of boats equipped with echosounders. This would either force N to one end of the lake, where it must finally appear in the shallows, or catch it as it passed through the sonar 'net'. Four boats, so equipped, made six sweeps both by day and by night (see Fig. 4). It was found that the sonar could be detected at

SWEEPING THE DEPTHS

Fig. 4: Diagram showing the technique used by the 1962 Cambridge University expedition to 'sweep' L Ness for N (from the *Observer*, 3 June 1962).

distances greater than 1.5 km. Consequently the 'net' must have covered the entire width of L Ness.

There was no evidence that the 'net' drove anything before it and in the six sweeps only one echo was obtained. This was just before a pole-like object was sighted in the same area. Later, using a silent searching technique (boat engine off), the expedition obtained two strong echoes, one off Foyers and one off Urquhart Castle. It was suggested that these contacts might have been large groups of salmon.[183] Six years later, the leader of the expedition (Baker[184]) claimed that nothing was detected by any of the boats.[185]

S6: 28 August 1968; University of Birmingham. In 1966 the Acoustics Division of the University's Department of Electronic and Electrical Engineering (Professor D. Gordon Tucker, Dr Hugh Braithwaite, Dr D. J. Creasey, *et al.)* began to develop a digital sonar system for use in the fishing industry. A digital system differs from the usual analogue system by having more compact circuits. It was a sector-searching sonar which was supposed to detect fish shoals up to 1.5 km away from the fishing vessel. Trials were conducted at L Ness in April and August

1968, and a test on 28 August appeared to detect some remarkable underwater movements which attracted world attention after publication of the results.[186]

The multibeam sonar, operating at 50 kHz, was located at Temple Pier (Drumnadrochit) and aimed straight across L Ness (3 km wide at that point). At a range of about 1.2 km a large stationary target was recorded, apparently in mid-water 75 m below the surface and extending for 50 m along the range axis. Tucker and Braithwaite declared that it might have been a waterlogged tree with other debris caught in it. Alternatively it might have been a large submerged rock face off Strone Point energized by the tertiary lobe of the horizontal diffraction pattern (caused by interference between the individual sonars). They did not know whether or not such a rock face existed.[187]

The sonars transmitted 1.5 ms pulses every 10 s (6 ppm), and the results were displayed on a CRO which was filmed by a cine camera. At 4.30 p.m. a large object appeared to rise from the bottom of the lake at 800 m range and approach the large fixed object; both objects produced about the same strength of signal. The moving target's velocity component along the axis of the sonar was not greater than 3 m/s and it appeared to have a vertical component of not greater than 0.5 m/s. A third target appeared to dive at 2.4 m/s while moving with a horizontal component of 7.5 m/s. This target had a length of several metres. Tucker and Braithwaite concluded that while the targets appeared to be animate, the high rate of ascent and descent made it unlikely that they were fish. They noted that it was tempting to suppose that the targets were N, but warned that a great deal more investigation was required with more refined equipment before any definite conclusions could be drawn. This did not prevent others from deriding their 'claims' to have found N, meanwhile making reasonable objections. It was alleged that a school of fish swimming through the sonar beam could give the impression of a rapidly diving object.[188] Burton (on television) proposed that the moving targets were otters.

More comprehensive tests were undertaken in September 1969 (in cooperation with Plessey), and in September 1970, but no more moving targets appeared. It was discovered that in the epilimnion the sonar could detect targets in excess of 1 km away. However, the steep thermal gradient of the thermocline caused refraction of the beam. The effect was to produce a 'shadow zone' between the two in which targets were invisible. At close range, divers could be detected at 120 m range and depths down to 30 m. But at medium and long ranges refraction made interpretation difficult; the bottom could be observed via a curved path, appearing to be in mid-water. Tucker and Creasey warned that the 1968 results (S6) were subject to reservations as a result of the discovery of refraction, and they were not certain that the discovered vertical velocities were real. Nevertheless they had confidence in the horizontal velocities, which indicated an animal. Separately Creasey observed that the mysterious objects observed in August 1968 were probably moving at a constant depth.[189]

We are left wondering what these fast-moving targets were. The failure to repeat the results does suggest that they were artefacts of the equipment. It is not impossible that there was an otter or a large fish in the area, but whatever it was, it does not rate as N without further evidence. Ignoring the caution and conditions imposed by the Birmingham team, Mackal made unwarranted deductions regarding the movement of large animals in L Ness and regarded the experiments as a 'rather spectacular success'.[190]

S7: 1969; Vickers Oceanics. Vickers the shipbuilders brought their six-man submarine *Pisces* to the lake, primarily to tow a model N for a film company. However, after the model sank, the submarine explored the depths. During one cruise, the vessel's sonar contacted what was taken to be a 'large moving target'. ITN reported skipper R. W. Easthaugh as follows:

A sonar target was picked up whilst *Pisces* was hovering 50 ft [15 m] off the bottom. The target was picked up at a distance of 600 ft [183 m]. *Pisces* homed on the target and when at a distance of 400 ft [122 m] the target rapidly disappeared from the screen. *Pisces* maintained its course and speed on the last heading, but no further contact was made. Nothing conclusive can be given [*sic*] upon this observation, nor have Vickers tried to do so – it is quoted here as an observation only. Depth of water: 520 ft [158.5 m]. Main channel: 300 yards [274 m] towards Inverness from Urquhart Castle. Observers: S. Boulton, T. Story, and B. Peach.

Mackal states that the sonar was a Western Marine Electronics SS100, operating at a frequency of 155 kHz. I have been unable to confirm this, or to obtain further details, such as the submarine's exact position, its course, or its speed.[191]

S8: 10 October 1969; Robert E. Love Jr. With a Honeywell 'Scanar' II-F sonar fitted in the motor vessel *Rangitea,* Love covered more than 256 km in 45 hours' patrolling. A cine camera took 20,000 frames of his sonar screen and its targets.

Love claims that on the above date, 2 km north-east of Foyers in mid-lake, he tracked a target which moved along a looped path 190 m long ahead and to one side of the boat, which was travelling on a straight course at a speed of 1.6 m/s. Love calculated that, on initial contact, the target was at least 67 m deep, and he also calculated that the target strength was equivalent to that of a volume of air of about 0.1–0.38 m³ which was compared by Mackal to the volume in the lungs of a 3 m pilot whale (0.04 m³).[192]

Inconsistencies in Love's data, particularly between the observation time and the boat's speed, coupled with the fact that his sonar could not give precise depths, have led to claims that he tracked inanimate debris. However, on ten subsequent searches of the area Love found nothing.

S9: 22 October 1970; Jeffrey Blonder. Contact was made with a target at 2.53 p.m. at a range of 274 m and a depth of 40 m near Invermoriston. No other data.[193]

S10: Autumn 1970; Academy of Applied Science. A short-range high-definition sidescan sonar designed by Klein was set up in Urquhart Bay (attached to an old pier support) where 'intruders' were seen to be moving through the sound beam underwater. One target was acquired on 21 September at 6.10 p.m. at 76 m range. The sonar was a Klein 'Hydroscan' MK-300 operated at 50 kHz and emitting a 0.1 ms pulse at a rate of 300 ppm in a beam 2° wide. It was set on a 200 m range scale.

Rines concluded that there are large moving objects in the lake, that there is abundant fish life which could support a large creature and that there are large ridges in the steep walls of the lake which could conceivably harbour large creatures.[194]

Due to inadequate data it is not possible to examine the claims for sonar contacts with large moving N. Rines's claims that they exist is unsubstantiated. The AAS has exhibited sonar charts which purport to show ridges. However, Mackal has pointed out that when the sidescan sonar is directed against a sloping surface, an echo will be returned where the slope is steep enough, but that with a shallow slope the signal will be reflected away from the transducer, producing no echo. He concluded therefore that the light and dark areas, which led the AAS team to conclude that they had discovered 'large ridges or caves'[195] are merely produced by variation in the slope of the bottom of L Ness.[196] This is a reasonable explanation for the variations in the sonar chart. Other surveys have found no evidence of ridges or caves, which in any case, considering the glacial scouring which the valley received during the last ice-age, are unlikely to exist.

S11: 8 August 1972; Academy of Applied Science. At the time that the AAS obtained underwater pictures (discussed in chapter 5) they deployed a sonar aimed horizontally so that it could detect objects moving within range of the camera-strobe. According to Rines, the sonar transducer was mounted on a stationary platform placed on the sloping bottom 10.5 m below the surface. The sonar system was a Raytheon DE-725C 'Explorer III' Fathometer Depth Sounder, which is normally used vertically. The recorder was in a boat (*Narwhal*) directly above the transducer. The camera-strobe was deployed from another boat (*Nan*).

Rines notes that at about 1 a.m., with the weather calm and the water flat, the team in *Narwhal* began to see 'the same kind of characteristic sonar traces obtained in 1970'[197] (see Plate XIX). He claimed that the chart showed an object at about 36.5 m range, but found that it did not show on any of the photographs. About 40 minutes later it was reported that salmon were seen jumping away from something in the water, and that this flight was seen on the sonar. At about the same time a large object came back into the sonar beam, and, a little later, a second object of similar size. Rines determined that the objects were about 3.6 m apart and claimed that the underwater photographs (U1/2/3) were obtained at this time.

The sonar chart was submitted to six 'experts' for interpretation, although the comments of only five have been published (see Plate XX). Two of the 'experts' were governors of the AAS and one of these two was a member of the team which obtained the recording. Rines summed up their view, that the tracing shows a large object with an appendage approximately 3 m long, and another large object separate from the first.[198] Personally, he believed that the parallel sonar traces were reflections from N's various parts when it was head-on to the transducer (i.e. reflections from head, front flipper, body, back flipper, etc.) and that a solid trace was from an N side-on to the transducer.[199]

Other accounts of the night's events have come from those who assisted Rines. Peter Davies of the LNIB, skipper of *Narwhal*, told Witchell that it had been quite choppy until about midnight when the wind dropped and the water settled to become calm. There were many fish (salmon) in the bay, and these appeared on the chart as tiny dots about the size of a pin head. About 1.45 a.m. the crew noticed that the fish dots were becoming streaks, as if the fish were all moving rapidly away from the area. Then a big black trace started to appear. Davies climbed into a tender (*Fussy Hen*) and paddled across to tell Rines in *Nan* what was happening. Davies, Rines, and Jan Willums then rowed quickly back to *Narwhal*, where the heavy trace was still visible. Then a slight breeze got up and *Narwal* started to swing around. At this point the dense trace disappeared.[200]

That the strong target was lost just as *Narwhal* swung about indicates that the sonar transducer was not on the bottom; it must have been suspended in mid-water below the boat. This is confirmed by one of the crew (Hilary Ross[201]), who states that it was suspended 4.5 m above the bottom, and by *Narwhal's* log[202] in which Davies noted that it was at a depth of 3.6 m. (These depths do not sum to the depth of water under the boat claimed by Rines.) Ross explained that the sonar transducer was attached to a length of timber approximately 1 m long which was slung diagonally beneath the boat so as to aim the transducer in the direction of *Nan*. Her recollection is that there was about 9 m of water beneath each boat and that the camera-strobe was on the bottom pointing towards *Narwhal*. She stated that there was deep water between the two boats. Raynor stated that *Nan* was moored in about 12 m of water, but on the edge of a steep slope (approx. 30°). He confirmed that *Narwhal* was moored only at the bow to a buoy which could move over a circle of radius 4.5 m. He advised me that *Nan*, being the lighter boat, responded readily to the wind. *Narwhal* on the other hand, being a heavier boat, tended to lie along the current until there was a strong wind. It could be expected therefore that in a light wind *Nan* would move while *Narwhal* would not. The extent to which *Nan*'s mooring could move is not known, but it may have been similar to that of *Narwhal*. The sonar chart must be viewed in a different light if it was possible for the transducer to rotate and for both boats to make independent movement. However, interpretation should not be attempted without full knowledge of the sonar system itself. Ross's account of the events includes the information that, at about 1.25 a.m., Davies sculled quietly in an inflatable (*sic*) to *Nan* and returned immediately with Rines (1.35 a.m.). There were no other boat movements in the immediate area.

The Explorer III echo-sounder had an unusual stylus arrangement in which three styli rotate one after the other, each recording consecutive depth phases, the depth depending on the mode. In this case the phases were each 45.72 m, but with the third phase inoperative because it was over the sonar's limit. However, all the styli marked the same chart and care was needed to discriminate between them. The sounder's manual explains that hard bottom can be distinguished from muddy bottom by the type of mark on the chart; hard surfaces cause the signal to bounce back and forth between the bottom and the surface producing a multiple trace (a series of parallel traces). A muddy bottom produces a single thick trace.

It can be seen that the chart (Plate XIX) exhibits both multiple traces and thick ones. It can also be seen (from Fig. 5) that the sounder was bound to catch *Nan* in its beam, and that it would do so intermittently as *Narwhal* swung about. Also, due to mooring slack (mainly on *Nan*), the distance between the two boats was not constant. It is evident that the multiple traces on the chart must be from *Nan*, the signal and a delayed echo showing 2nd-time returns. Even the trace at 1.45 starts off with multiples and so must be from *Nan*. Unfortunately, a few minutes later, just after *Nan* was pulled back by its mooring rope, the sounder picked

Plate XIX: The sonar chart for S11. Distances are marked in feet, with the origin at the top. Time increases from left to right, and the strong arcs show 5 min. intervals (*author's collection; copyright Academy of Applied Science*).

up a distant bottom echo (which is also evident elsewhere on the chart) and merged it with the trace from *Nan*. The marks on the chart which the AAS claim are evidence of N are entirely and necessarily explicable as signals from the boats involved and parts of the bottom of Urquhart Bay. There is no evidence that the photographic evidence (U1/2/3) is at all related to this sonar evidence.

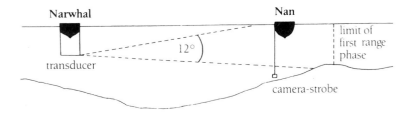

Fig. 5: Scale section of the relative positions of *Narwhal* and *Nan* and the sonar transducer, showing how *Nan* must have been caught in the sonar beam.

S12/13: 1976; Academy of Applied Science. In an article published in 1976, Klein and Finkelstein announced the detection of 'moving objects' in L Ness by means of sidescan sonar mounted at Temple Pier.[203] It was implied that these objects were N.

An EG & G Mark 1B sonar was attached to a metal frame and placed on the bottom beside the Pier and aimed out towards a camera-strobe array 55 m away and 8 m below the surface (suspended from a raft). The sonar operated at 105 kHz and had a pulse length of 0.1 ms; its beam was 2.4° wide by 20° or 50° high depending on the mode. The sonar recorder and its CRO were mounted in a caravan on Temple Pier. The sonar was set to a range of 200 m, but it was effective to only 145 m. The camera-strobe appeared as a continuous thick trace at 55 m range. At 10.44 p.m. on 30 June 1976 the sonar recorded the approach of a target (see Plate XXIa) which was picked up at 180 m. It slowed and stopped for about 1 minute at 140 m range (80 m from the camera), and then departed at about the same speed as on its approach (velocity was not stated). As can be seen, not only has someone noted the position of the camera (with an arrow and a dashed line), but the word 'Hunter' has been written against the anomalous trace. *Hunter is* a cruiser used by Rines in the 1975 expedition; it may indeed have been used in this expedition, although it has only been admitted that *Malaran* was employed. If the trace could at the time be identified as *Hunter* and there is no alternative to this explanation, it is a mystery why Wyckoff should later have written 'Nessiteras Rhombopteryx?' on the chart. Such a fancy does not seem to be justified.

On 30 June a second transducer (the other half of the 1B) was added to provide a horizontal beam perpendicular to that of the first transducer. At 5.15 a.m. the following day a trace started at about 170 m range and, with a slight variation, gradually increased range for a short time (unspecified) until it disappeared (see Plate XXIb). On the chart it is recorded that this contact was made by the horizontal beam, and someone has noted that the target was over 9 m deep. This estimate of depth was probably deduced from the fact that the beam was aimed at the camera-strobe, which was 8 m deep. However, it cannot have been easy to aim the beam exactly at the camera, and we do not know the depth of the transducers. If it is assumed that the transducers were at the same depth as the camera (as seems to be indicated by the plan published in the article), then the horizontal-beam transducer only had to be aimed 1.5° high to catch a surface object at 170 m range (see Fig. 6). That the object was a boat is also indicated by what the authors call 'filaments', the multiple traces typical of false echoes from 2nd- and 3rd-time returns from a hard surface. The sudden appearance of the boat in the beam can have been due to the fact that when it was closer it was outside the beam angle.

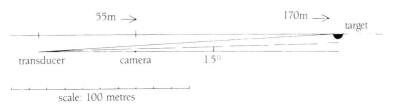

Fig. 6: Scale section showing how the horizontal sidescan sonar could 'see' a surface target at 170 m range. Bottom profile not shown.

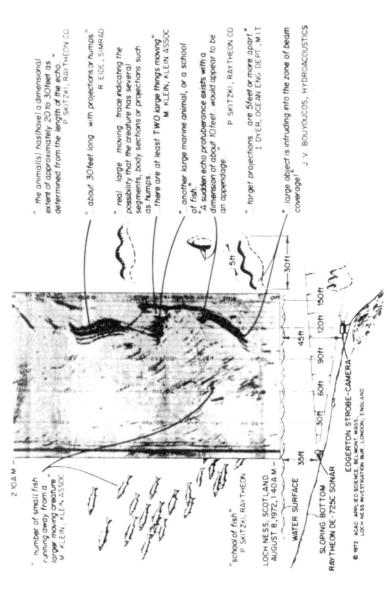

" the animal(s) has(have) a dimensional
extent of approximately 20 to 30feet as
determined from the length of the echo..."
                    P SKITZKI, RAYTHEON CO

"...about 30feet long...with projections or humps..."
                              R EIDE, SIMRAD

"...real, large, moving, trace indicating the
possibility that the creature has several
segments, body sections or projections such
as humps.
...there are at least TWO large things moving"
                    M KLEIN, KLEIN ASSOC

"...another large marine animal, or a school
of fish."
"A sudden echo protuberance exists with a
dimension of about 10feet...would appear to be
an appendage..."
                    P SKITZKI, RAYTHEON CO

"...target projections...are 5feet or more apart."
                    I DYER, OCEAN ENG DEPT, MIT

"...large object is intruding into the zone of beam
coverage!"
                    J V BOUYOUCOS, HYDROACOUSTICS

2 10 A M —

" number of small fish
running away from a
larger moving creature "
    M KLEIN, KLEIN ASSOC

"school of fish"
    P SKITZKI, RAYTHEON

LOCH NESS, SCOTLAND
AUGUST 8, 1972, 1·40 A M —

WATER SURFACE   35ft

SLOPING BOTTOM
RAYTHEON DE-725C SONAR

EDGERTON STROBE-CAMERA
© 1972 ACAD APPLIED SCIENCE, BELMONT, MASS.
    LOCH NESS INVESTIGATION BUR., LONDON, ENGLAND

5ft   30ft

30ft 60ft 90ft 120ft 150ft

45ft

Plate XX: Interpretation of the S11 chart by some 'experts' (*author's collection: copyright Academy of Applied Science*).

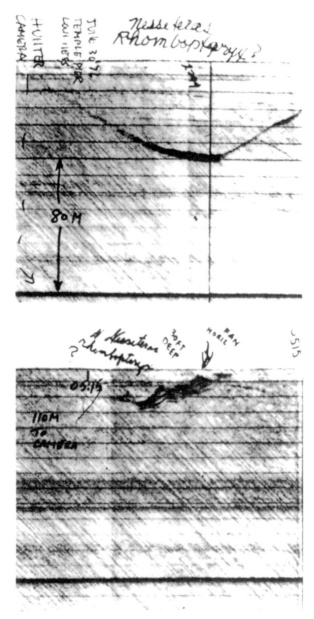

Plate XXI: (a) Top, sonar chart for S12; distance increases vertically, with the origin off the chart at the bottom, and time increases left to right. (b) Bottom, sonar chart for S13; distance and time scale as for S12 (*Author's collection; copyright Academy of Applied Science*).

As it departed it fell into the beam at 170 m, only to disappear when it exceeded the limit of the sonar. It has not been stated that there were no boat movements at the time these traces were obtained. In June 1997, the AAS returned with sidescan sonar but have published no results.

S15: 1978; Theo Brown. Brown was an expert in shark repellent methods, both in Australia and Tahiti for the French Government's Institute of Medical Research and the French Polynesian Fishery Service. In 1978 the World Life Research Institute, a United States Government-sponsored body based in California, asked him to put his expertise to work in L Ness. He arrived in July but was only able to go on the water for a few days in eight weeks due to bad weather. From a small inflatable boat he suspended underwater loudspeakers through which he relayed tape-recorded signals, at the same time scanning the lake with sonar.

> Suddenly I got lucky. I was about a mile [1.6 km] south-west of Foyers where the loch is about 700 ft [213 m] deep when I definitely got a response from a large animal moving up from very deep water into range of my sonar. It held itself at levels varying between 200 and 215 ft [61–65.5 m] below the surface. I had contact with it for about one-and-three-quarter [*sic*] minutes and, by pure rotten luck, a large boat came along and the sound of its motor caused the creature to move off fast. I now have a clear sonar graph showing a solid animate mass between 30 and 50 ft [9–15 m] long and from six to nine ft [2–3 m] in depth, and it is going to be subjected to interpretive examination when I go home next week.
>
> I have a lot of taped sounds to work with, but because of bad weather conditions, I got nowhere near to trying them all. But at the time of my successful contact in Loch Ness, I was using one which works well with large marine predators. I know now there is something large living in the loch.

Brown explained that part of the transmitted signal was 'infra-sonic', at a frequency below the human range of hearing. A crude comparison was the sound made by a wounded fish when it moved its body to create low frequency distress signals. It was reported that Brown had made a copy of his chart available to Rines for examination.[204]

S16: April 1981; Provider II. Early in April 1981, brothers Robert and James West of Fraserburgh were on L Ness in their 15 m fishing boat. The boat was fitted with a Koden CVS886 Mk II Colour Sounder with a 28 kHz transducer directing a 31.6° beam vertically downwards. Different strengths of echo are displayed in different colours on its CRO screen. They claimed that as they were testing the echo-sounder they detected a 'weird shape' below the boat at a depth of 55 m. A newspaper report stated that the object was 18 m long, 9 m wide, and with a tapering neck and hump back, but one of the brothers pointed out that the size is not easily calculated from the equipment (nor is the shape for that matter). The object was tracked for three minutes in water that was 140 m deep at that point (between Lochend and Urquhart Bay).[205] They claimed that the sonar showed that the object was not a shoal of fish, but Marconi International Marine, who market Koden, state that the orange display which the Wests obtained, although it indicates a strong echo, can be obtained from fish shoals if they are dense. The sonar was new and perhaps unfamiliar to the Wests. Although they promised me that on future journeys through L Ness they would keep the sonar on, 'freezing' the picture for later analysis, I have not heard from them again. It seems likely that the Wests have learned to recognise fish shoals.

S17/18: 1981–85; Loch Ness and Morar Project. In 1979 The Loch Morar Expedition became The Loch Ness and Morar Project (incorporating the remnants of The Loch Morar Survey and the LNIB) and returned to L Ness using sonar, evidence from all other methods having been dismissed. The objective was to repeat previous sonar contacts and to establish some pattern leading perhaps to active underwater photography. Using a purpose-built sonar research vessel (*John Murray*), 1981 was spent testing equipment and devising operating procedures, but during August some sonar contacts were made. These were all rated inconclusive.

From the beginning of May to the end of August 1982 two searchlight sonars were operated for over 1500 hours in day and night patrols of the northern basin. They were mounted on a barge (*Phyllis*) and a motor cruiser (*New Atlantis*). The sonar was calibrated to detect targets stronger than a 330 g fish at a depth of 150 m, and only contacts below 30 m were tracked. A total of forty such contacts were made, including single targets of considerable strength, but it was not possible to eliminate the possibility that they were inanimate objects, freak side wall returns, or even larger fish.

In 1983 the Project attempted to repeat these results, but with some additional controls. Although contacts were obtained in mid-water, controls were still not satisfactory and no results were published.[206]

For 1984 an inflatable raft fitted with sonar was securely anchored in 213 m of water opposite Horseshoe Scree. This ensured that if targets showed movement they really were moving. Although a few contacts were made with moving targets down to 50 m depth, their low strength was consistent with them being large fish.

On 9 and 10 October 1987 two partial sonar sweeps (Operation Deepscan) were conducted using twenty small launches equipped with Lowrance X-16 sonars. Although some mid-water contacts were made they were not identified, nor thought to be very large animals.

S19: 1992; Simrad. At 7.04 p.m. on 28 July 1992, sidescan sonar on the MV *Simrad,* operating on behalf of Project Urquhart, an exploration sponsored by several scientific institutions and organised by author and newscaster Nicholas Witchell, obtained a strong two-minute contact with an unidentified target near Invermoriston. Unfortunately the event was not recorded and the exact position of the ship was not noted. Most likely the target was a reflection from the walls or bottom of the lake.

Negative Sonar Evidence

In May 1969, David James and the LNIB were joined by Major Eustace Maxwell, Lord Richard Percy, and Ian Lyster in a sonar search aboard the drifter *Penorva.* They employed a Marconi Depth Sounder, a Raytheon 729 Fathometer and a Seascribe Depth Finder. They found no sign of N.[207]

In September 1969 ITN sponsored Plessey to conduct experiments using their Model 195 sonar which operated at the low frequency of 10 kHz. The system was designed for long range use in the open sea and its use in the confines of L Ness produced what Mackal called an 'auditory shambles'. The frequency is well within the range of human hearing, and with an output of 5 kW the pulse transmitted into the water could be heard by observers along the shore. These intense sound pulses were reflected and redirected throughout the lake, rendering the target display virtually useless.[208] N did not respond to this noise.

From 25 July to 16 September 1983, Rikki Razdan and Alan Kielar of Iscan Inc. from Rochester, New York, deployed 15 tonnes of equipment in a hunt for N. This equipment consisted of 144 sonar transducers and nine biopsy-sampling devices arrayed in a grid 24.5 m square with 2.1 m between each device. The transducers, with a beam of only about 2°, and a range of only 30 m, acted as triggers for the biopsy system. The grid was moored to the AAS raft in Urquhart Bay and monitored from the chalet on Temple Pier. The sonar returns were displayed on a CRO marked with the grid, and capable of showing ten different colours related to the depth of the target. The sampling darts could be fired manually or automatically if any object interrupted the beam of several transducers at once. There was also a recording system. During the eight weeks of observation there was no sign of N.[209]

The Evidence from Hydrophones

There have been several reports that hydrophones in L Ness have detected anomalous or unidentified sounds. In 1962 a team led by H. G. Hasler recorded several low-frequency tapping noises 'which seemed animal-like in nature',[210] although they had no evidence that they were caused by an animal. Ike Blonder of the AAS recorded some clicking sounds, the source of which was never identified;[211] Dinsdale states that these sounds were double 5 ms bursts in the 4–8 kHz range and suggested that they might be from an animal sonar.[212]

In 1970 Mackal and his team built and deployed several complex hydrophones, but the results were inconclusive. He did not obtain any sounds that could be identified with large aquatic creatures, although he described some 'bird-like chirps'. On the evening of 28 October 1970, a hydrophone detected mysterious clicks that appeared to come from near the surface and were not traced to any surface activity. Later these sounds were detected all over Urquhart Bay, but no pattern could be found and the source was not identified. In addition, near the end of their 1970 programme, the team heard loud 'knocks' spaced at irregular intervals a second or more apart. These noises were sometimes accompanied by a turbulent 'swishing', and they all faded when a motor boat approached the hydrophone. Mackal did not reveal whether or not his recordings of these sounds were played to an expert, such as Dr Hassler of the University of Wisconsin, who identified some sounds he obtained in L Michigan, and his failure to do so is surprising. He did state that 'competent authorities [unnamed] state that one of the known forms of life in the loch [not listed] has the anatomical capabilities of producing such calls'.[213]

Using hydrophones during their 1961 survey expedition, the team from the University of Birmingham heard neither fish nor other noises at frequencies up to 60 kHz.[214]

In January 2000, two Swedish cryptozoologists, Jan-Ove Sundberg and Goran Rajala, came with hydrophones and a large net to capture N. They claimed to have recorded strange sounds on Lake Seljordsvatnet, which they interpreted as coming from the lake's reputed inhabitant: Selma. They did not catch or find any sign of N.

The Radar Evidence

As might be expected, radar is not very useful for N-hunting. N rarely surfaces. There have been no systematic radar searches, and only one incidental report.

On 22 August 1966 it was reported that the motor-yacht *Pharma* had tracked N on its radar for nearly half an hour after it was first seen. Observers reported seeing five humps about 1 km astern. Capt. J. Gough of Bridlington said 'What I saw has me completely puzzled. It looked like the belly of a huge horse breaking the surface'. G. Ralph of Inverness, the pilot, watched N on the radar scanner. 'It was sharp in the nose and tapered to a point at the other end. The part above the water measured about 30 feet [9 m]'.[215] Witchell's claim that this yacht was owned by the British Medical Association[216] has not been confirmed.

7

The Evidence from Lakes
other than Loch Ness

It has long been noticed that L Ness is not the only Scottish lake reported to be inhabited by N or its kind, and that Scotland is not the only country to have lakes in which monsters are reported. Almost every lake in Scotland has its attributed monster and many temperate zone lakes in other countries are also alleged to be so occupied. However, the exceptions are curious. How is it that not one of the many lakes in the English Lake District has a reputation for monsters and that the Swiss lakes lack such aquatic marvels?

Reports of monsters in other lakes have been used to support the case for N. However, as I have noted, these reports may have been stimulated by the reports from L Ness, and a circular argument may exist. Nevertheless we can examine this evidence, even though conclusions regarding the existence of such monsters depend on the conclusion regarding N.

The Bords list 265 lakes with reports of monsters (although some of their Scottish lakes are firths).[217] I shall deal only with those lakes where either there has been some instrumental evidence or there has been a serious attempt at investigation. This may involve mention of eyewitness accounts in those cases.

Reports from Other Scottish Lakes

The reports come mainly from the more remote and deep lakes such as Morar and Shiel, but reports have also come from Lomond (the lake with the largest surface area), Rannoch, Tay, and Arkaig. However, investigation has been sparse. About 1850 the owner of L Beiste (on Greenstone Point in Wester Ross) drained it in an attempt to capture its monster. When this failed, he tried to poison the beast with quick lime; that also failed. In 1870 an attempt was made to catch the monster reported to inhabit L nan Dubhrachan on the Sleat in Skye by dragging it with a long net. All that was caught were two pike.[218]

Apart from L Ness, serious investigation has been attempted only at L Morar, the deepest lake in Scotland. In her book, Montgomery Campbell lists thirty-three separate eyewitness reports of the monster in L Morar (which I shall call M). This is one famous example.

At between 9 and 9.30 p.m. on 16 August 1969, Duncan McDonell and William Simpson were returning from a fishing trip in their cabin cruiser. Although the sun had set, there was still daylight and the surface of the lake was dead calm. As they were approaching the islands at the western end of the lake at a speed of about 3 m/s, McDonell heard a splash and disturbance astern. Looking round he saw a 'creature' approaching directly behind in their wake. In only a few seconds it caught up and grazed the side of the boat, after which it stopped or slowed. McDonnell grabbed an oar to fend it off, but the oar was old and it broke. Simpson described how the animal surfaced behind the boat, colliding with such an impact that a kettle of water was knocked to the floor. Seeing the oar break, he grabbed his rifle and fired at the beast. It slowly sank away from the boat, but neither man saw any blood or other sign that the creature had been hit. They estimated that the visible length was between 8 and 9 m with three humps about 45 cm out of the water. Later McDonell said that they were undulations rather than humps. The skin was rough and dirty brown in colour. They saw no tail but McDonell described the top of a snake-like head, brown in colour, about 30 cm across the top and about 45 cm out of the water, but with no visible features.[219]

Mackal attempted an investigation by examining the boat for animal tissue, but he found nothing but scratches (which might have been there beforehand). He compared McDonell's description (which he expanded) to that of a monkfish, which he claimed reaches lengths of up to 2.4 m. (such fish are found in the sea around Mallaig, although there is no reason to think they would enter L Morar). According to Mackal's account the cruiser was travelling at 7 m/s and it collided with the surfacing M.[220]

An event that occurred after Montgomery Campbell's book was published produced the following report. On 3 March 1981, Sydney Wignall, an international explorer and archaeologist, Dr Bryan Woodward of the University of Loughborough, and John Evans, a professional photographer, were returning to the western end of the lake in a rigid-hulled inflatable at about 2.5 m/s (due to a leak which prevented the usual speed of 10 m/s). The time was about 3.30 p.m. and the water was flat calm. They were about mid-lake west of Brinacory Island when they noticed two humps or projections standing out of the water and travelling in the same direction as the boat at between 1.5 and 2 m/s.

These humps were some 100 m astern and about 20 m off to starboard, the first one being about 1.2 m long and about 30 cm high and slightly triangular in shape. The rear protuberance was separated by about a metre from the first and was described as being the size and shape of a human hand held upright out of the water. Both objects were black. Wignall slowed the boat and turned to starboard, but at less than 75 m the objects disappeared. It was agreed that the objects had been in sight for between 17 and 20 seconds. The following day tests failed to show that the boat's wake could produce such humps. It was thought that the object had been too big to be an otter.[221]

The Loch Morar Survey, of which Montgomery Campbell was a committee member, mounted expeditions in 1970, 1971 and 1972. These were to study the ecology of the lake and to try to obtain evidence of M by filming or other methods. In 1973 the Survey announced that it had collected 37 'apparently authentic' reports, mostly from recent years and that the descriptions agreed with those from L Ness. Although Survey members reported four visual sightings, attempts to obtain film of M were unsuccessful. Nor were there any positive results from the use of hydrophones in 1972.[222]

In 1974 Adrian Shine arrived at Morar with a submersible observation chamber (*Machan*) which he had designed and built. This enabled an observer to monitor the surface from the bottom, the idea being that any M would be seen in silhouette. Results were negative. In 1975 Shine, with students from Royal Holloway College, spent six weeks at L Morar scanning the entire perimeter of the lake to a depth of 10 m using *Pequod*, a specially designed glass fibre boat with a transparent dome in the bow through which the bottom could be observed. No evidence or remains of M were found.[223]

The Loch Morar Survey submitted two of their reports (Sween MacDonald, 8 August 1971; Johnson/Binns, 10 August 1971) to the Scottish headquarters of the Nature Conservancy Council for comment. The reply stated that whereas several alternative explanations might be suggested, it was not possible to give a definite opinion, and it was thought to be extremely unscientific to try to hazard a guess of the cause of either incident. Despite this advice, Montgomery Campbell concluded that 'something' very much faster and more powerful than an otter had caused the reports.[224]

Reports from Irish Lakes

Although strange creatures are reported to inhabit many Irish lakes (an unsurprising fact considering the close cultural links between Scotland and Ireland), little investigation has been made. In May 1966 (or 1965 according to Mackal) Captain Lionel Leslie and Lord Massarene, together with a friend and three marine biologists, attempted to capture the monster which was reported to inhabit L Fadda near Clifden. Their method was to explode gelignite underwater, filming the result. Although a strange disturbance was observed after the explosion, this was not filmed and no monster appeared. In 1968 another attempt was made to trap the animal, but this time in an adjoining lake, which Mackal, who was present, identifies as L Nahooin. A net was stretched across the lake and an electronic fish stunner employed. Nothing appeared.[225]

Reports from Scandinavian Lakes

There were many reports of a monster in L Suldal, a long narrow mountain lake in the Rogoland district of Norway. The creature was said to be the size of a small island, coloured grey-brown and slimy. Others said that it was shining black with some white, about the size of a four-oared boat, with a head pointed like a bellows and with large eyes. In the summer of 1892 the local school inspector, A. J. Olsen, who was also president of the directors of the Stavanger Museum, visited the lake to investigate the reports. He found that most reports were made when the weather was warm and the lake calm. The water would begin to boil and seethe, after which a large dark body shaped like a capsized boat would appear. After splashing up and down for some minutes, the object would sink out of sight. Olsen concluded that the monster was no more than sawdust from the two sawmills at the head of the lake; after settling on the bed of the lake and covered in slime, the sawdust fermented and burst up to the surface. This hypothesis was not accepted by the local people, who demanded a full inquiry. Such an inquiry was held, allowing all the local witnesses to give evidence. However, the Museum refused to finance an expedition to capture the monster. The next year the local schoolteacher and his brother were out in a boat on the lake when they noticed strange movements on the surface. There was a lot of foam and what appeared to be a large log. The water seethed in several places and an object like an upturned boat swayed backwards and forwards, slowly sinking until only a small part was visible. After rowing over to the spot, the brothers discovered that the objects were a mass of sawdust, halfrotten plants, pine needles, pieces of wood and mud from the bottom of the lake. The first published accounts of monsters in Norwegian lakes appear to have coincided with the construction of sawmills on the mountain streams.[226]

L Storsjo, a deep lake in the mountains of central Sweden, is reported to contain a monster. Dr Peter Olsson, a zoology teacher at Ostersund State High School, who lived on the lakeside, first heard reports in the 1890s. He uncovered some twenty-two reports from 1820 to 1898. For instance, about 1839 Aron Andersson from Hackas, with some others, saw an animal swimming out from the shore into the open lake. It appeared similar to a sort of grey-red horse with a white mane. Suddenly it disappeared in deep water. Another report, in 1863, came from the Bromee family, who saw a creature splashing about on a beach. It had short thick feet (legs?), and when chased in the water it appeared like 10–12 ducks scooting along the surface one after the other. The 'ducks' were like shiny black humps. In another report, from 1873, an animal with a dog-like head swam at great speed following a boat. There were many reports of a shape like 'an upturned boat'. In 1894 an experienced Norwegian whaler was hired to catch the monster, but he never saw it once in a whole year. Olsson, who thought it was the giant seal described by Oudemans, published his views and evidence in 1899. Reports continue along the same lines, but Swedish zoologists attribute them to the effects of alcohol.[227]

Reports from Icelandic Lakes

Iceland's lake monsters are called *skimsl*, and they are reported from several lakes. The *skrimsl* of Skoradalsvatn was described as 13 m long with a head and neck 2 m high, a body 6 m long, and a tail 5 m long. It was seen by a farmer at Grund floating and playing on the surface for half an hour. The *skrimsl* of Lagarfljot, a long freshwater mountain lake in eastern Iceland, is described as being the size of a large vessel and moving rapidly. There are reports of one hump, with signs of a tail, and also of three humps which remained for a whole day.[228] An Icelandic scholar, Dr Hjaltalin, described in 1860 how he had been shown a mass of flesh and bones which had been washed up on a beach of the Lagarfljot. He said that the bones were quite different from those of a whale and that he was unable to identify them as those of any marine animal known to exist in the northern seas.[229] When, in 1980, the Icelandic Museum of Natural History was asked about these bones, it stated that the Lagarfljotsormur (*sic*) had never been anything but a legend and that all that had been seen were leaves, branches, and vegetable matter brought together by strong currents in the Lagafljot river.[230]

Reports from North American Lakes

Many Canadian lakes are the source of legends of monsters, the legends originating with the aboriginal peoples. For instance, Indian legends describe a beast which is supposed to inhabit L Utopia, near St George, New Brunswick. Yet it was 1967 before a white man (A. Seith Adams) reported seeing it. Lumbermen employed at a sawmill on the lake repeatedly observed a creature 9 m long splashing about in the lake, and attempts were made to catch it with baited hooks. The last recorded sighting was by a Mrs McKillop, who reported that a huge creature looking like a black rock had emerged from the water, moving and churning it. There is no good photographic evidence, but the New Brunswick Museum in St John has a sketch made by one B. Kroupa.[231]

Since the 1920s there have been reports of a monster in L Pohenegamook (a name derived from the Indian word for a monster) in Quebec. In 1977 it was alleged that this monster was tracked for ten days by a three-man team of divers with sonar equipment. They claimed to have acquired a 7.6 m trace from 'right under their boat' and a black shape in a picture taken by one of their automatic cameras.[232] Mackal confirms that investigation has involved divers and sonar, and that the sonar detected an object 8 m long. He states that the most recent sightings have been investigated by Dr Vadim Vladykov, a marine biologist and director of the Quebec Department of Game and Fisheries, who has concluded that 'there definitely is a strange, large animal living in Lake Pohenegamook'.[233]

Perhaps the most famous lake monster in Canada is Ogopogo (O) who is reported to live in L Okanagan, near the US border in British Columbia. Although about the same depth as L Ness, it is much longer (125 km) and wider (3 km). Due to being at greater elevation (350 m) and further from the sea (250 km) it is colder (1–2°C). Reports of a monster in the lake originated with the Indians in the late seventeenth century, but there have been some 200 reports from 1700 to the present day. Most reports date from the 1870s when Susan Allison saw what she thought was a log suddenly swim up-lake against the wind.[234] In 1914 the rotting carcase of a strange animal was found washed up on one of the beaches. It was 1.5–1.8 m long, with a round head, flippers, and a broad tail, was blue-grey in colour and weighed 180 kg. Local naturalists identified it as a manatee (sea cow), but it was a long way from its natural environment. Unfortunately the neck was missing, which raised a question as to how the head came to be with the body.[235] In July 1926 John L. Logie and family paced what they thought was O for several kilometres along the west shore of a dead calm lake north of Penticton. They could still see the paddle steamer *Sicamous*, which had left on its northward run an hour earlier.[236] Arthur Folden, a sawmill worker, was driving his wife north from Penticton on a sunny day in August 1968 when they noticed something large and lifelike moving through the calm-water south of Peachland. Thinking it was O, Folden stopped the car and reached for his 8 mm cine camera. He was fairly high above the water and about 300 m from the shore; the object which he filmed for 1 minute was about 200 m from the shore. For a year and a half the film was seen only by friends in private, but on 2 February 1970 it was shown to several Kelowna officials. Later the film was shown to civic leaders, businessmen, representatives of the Fish and Game Department of the government, and the news media. The object surfaced and submerged three times while travelling several hundred metres; it was obviously neither a boat nor a log. But not everyone was convinced that it was an animal; sceptics pointed to the delay in making the film public and the fact that Folden had added a shot of the sign, about 2.5 km north from where the film was shot, which reads 'Ogopogo's Lair'. Subsequently both Folden and his film disappeared and the location of neither is known,[237] but Clarke's book contains a colour still from the film.[238] On 3 August 1976 Ed Fletcher from Vancouver was out on the lake between 1 and 2 p.m. when something in the water cut across his bow. He said, 'If I hadn't shut the engine off I could have run him over or jumped on his back. The boat drifted to within 30 ft [9 m] of him.' Fletcher and his daughter, Diane, who was with him in the boat, were close enough to the shore at Gellatly Bay to turn back and fetch their camera. They came back out with another passenger, Gary Slaughter of Kelowna, and almost on cue, says Fletcher, O surfaced again. 'I saw his whole length this time, about 70-75 ft [21–23 m]. I shut the engine off when we got near him, and the boat coasted to within 50 ft [15 m] of him when I shot the first picture.' For an hour, the three watched. 'He would submerge, swim at least two city blocks, then surface and all the while we chased after him. The creature surfaced and submerged more than a dozen times and Fletcher took five photographs. He claimed that it swam coiled up and then stretched out, but even coiled up it was 12 m long. Diane Fletcher described the skin as smooth and brownish like that of a whale, with small ridges on its back. It swam in an undulating manner, turning like a corkscrew. Both she and Slaughter thought that the head was 60 cm or more long, flattened like that of a snake and with two projections like the ears of a 'Dobermann Pinscher'. Moon's book shows one of Fletcher's photographs.[239] Between April 1977 and August 1978 newspapers around L Okanagan carried a dozen reports, often from confirmed sceptics. Harry Staines of Westbank said, 'I did not believe it before, but we circled the thing in our boat, keeping it about a hundred yards [91 m] away.' He described it as resembling a long black eel about 11 m long, swimming with an up-and-down motion and leaving 'quite a wake'. In 1977 sixty volunteer scuba divers took turns to be lowered in a cage 9 m down into the lake. They were equipped with cameras and powerful aircraft landing lights in order to photograph O. This plan failed, but later there was a plan to lower electrodes into the water in the hope of stimulating an appearance. A L Okanagan Investigation Bureau has been established, but it has produced little more than a constant stream of eyewitness reports. The Federation of British Columbia

Naturalists described the cause of these reports as 'an optical illusion produced when an observer views obliquely a bow wave moving across flat water under certain lighting conditions.'[240] Moon reports that no attempt has been made to locate O with sonar.[241] Mackal believes that there is a small population of aquatic fish-eating animals in the lake, and identifies them as primitive whales of the group archeoceti.[242] In fact Mackal believes that some type of protowhale travels over the extensive Canadian river and lake system.

Part of that system are L Manitoba and L Winnipegosis north of Winnipeg. The monster believed to inhabit these two lakes, which are joined by the Dauphin River, is called Manipogo (presumably in imitation of O). It was not reported by white men until 1935. Most descriptions are of a flat, snake-like head, dark skin, and three humps. It is even reported to have a mate and young. Steve Rehaluk of Rorkton, Manitoba, his wife Ann, and his two sons were sitting at a picnic table when there was a ripple in the water. 'When I first looked there was only one. But when I ran to the shore I could see another beside it and a third trailing behind.' He thought that they looked like three big black snakes.[243] Professor R. K. Stewart-Hay of the University of Manitoba concluded that they had seen a swimming musk-rat followed by its young. On 12 August 1962 news commentator Richard Vincent was out in a fishing boat with John Konefall when they spotted an object about 300 m away. It looked like a large black snake or eel about 30 cm in girth (sic) and about 3.6 m long. One of them took a photograph from a distance of between 45 and 70 m (see Fig. 7), a copy of which can be seen in Costello's book. Although the boat had an outboard motor they could not keep up with the 'monster'.[244] Interviewed recently, neither Vincent nor Konefall would admit involvement. There is a story that in the 1930s a bone was dredged up from the bed of L Manitoba, but that subsequently it was lost in a fire. However, there is a wooden replica, which resembles a spinal vertebra about 15 cm long and 7 cm wide. Costello suggested that it was made by someone with access to a large museum, and Professor J. A. McLeod, former head of the Department of Zoology at the University of Manitoba, thought that it was a replica of a bone from a long-extinct animal. Beginning in 1960, McLeod led a number of unsuccessful searches for remains.[245] Professors Lehn and Schroeder (also of the University) found that under certain conditions (cold water with warm air) mirages occurred on L Winnipeg, and that in particular

Fig. 7: A sketch of the 'monster' shown in the Vincent/Konefall photograph. The photographer has not identified himself.

a boulder on one shore appeared to be a merman (or a 'monster') from the other shore over 1 km away.[246] Although such a situation must also occur on L Manitoba/Winnipegosis, it is not yet clear that any of the monster reports describe anything resembling a mirage.

According to Mackal there are no substantiated water monsters in the popular sense in American (sic) lakes, and Costello noted that no photographs, drawings, or remains supported the eyewitness accounts[247] (but see below). As Mackal noted, the best case is that made for the existence of a monster in L Champlain in Vermont. 'Champ' was first reported by Samuel de Champlain (after whom the lake was named) in 1609, when he described a 6 m long snake-like creature with a horselike head. Mackal knew of 27 collected reports covering the period from 1819 to the present; he thought that two were hoaxes, six were of known animals, and nineteen were unexplained.[248] Today the L Champlain Phenomena Investigation Bureau (formed and run by Joseph W Zarzynski) has over 200 reports on its files, and knows of several photographs and cine films. The pre-eminent photograph is that taken by Sandra Mansi in 1977 (shown in Zarzynski's book). However, Mansi took only one photograph, did not immediately report the incident, lost the negative, and cannot now locate the site. Analysis by one expert suggests that there was a sand-bar just below the surface (implying hoax), while another, by making some questionable assumptions about wind speed, water depth, and length of fetch, concluded that the object was between 4.8 and 17.2 m long. There have been some sonar explorations but the results are inconclusive.[249]

A long list of monster reports, first from the Indians and later (1885 onwards) from steamboat crews, originates at Flathead L, Montana. This is the largest lake in the north-west USA, being 43 km long by 24 km wide. There has been no scientific investigation, although skin divers have searched and some have attempted to capture the monster by baiting. All results have been negative.[250]

A report of a strange creature in Alkali L, near May Springs, Nebraska, reached the New York Times in July 1923. The issue of 25 July reported that J. A. Johnson and two companions had gone to the lake to camp and hunt. Early in the morning, walking around the shore, they suddenly came upon an animal nearly three-quarters out of the shallow water 18 m from them.

> The animal was probably forty feet [12 m] long, including the tail and the head, when raised in alarm as when he saw us. In general appearance the animal was not unlike an alligator, except that the head was stubbier, and there seemed to be a projection like a horn between the eyes and nostrils. The animal was built much more heavily throughout than an alligator. Its colours seemed a dull grey or brown.

There was a very distinctive and somewhat unpleasant odor noticeable for several moments after the beast had vanished into the water. We stood for several minutes after the animal had gone, hardly knowing what to do or say, when we noticed several hundred feet out from shore a considerable commotion in the water.

Sure enough the animal came to the surface, floated there a moment and then lashed the water with its tail, suddenly dived and we saw no more of him.

Mackal identified this animal as an elephant seal.[251]

An ingenious hoax was perpetrated at Silver L, Wyoming County, New York. On the evening of 13 July 1855 a group of 'honest, temperate and industrious' men and boys, who were out fishing, sighted an 18 m-long creature which, they alleged, chased them to shore. They described it as a serpent 18–30 m long, shiny, dark green with yellow spots, flaming red eyes, a mouth and huge fins. Thousands visited the village of Perry and expeditions were mounted. Two years later, as the result of a fire, the hoax was discovered. Two people confessed that they had built the monster out of waterproof canvas, paint and wire, and that it was towed by ropes and made to surface by pumping in air.[252] Mackal lists twenty-eight other US lakes with monster reports.[253]

Reports from Japan

Lake monsters have even reached Japan. Issie, the favourite, in L Ikeda, has two humps and has already earned a Mr Matsubara 100,000 yen when he won the money offered by Ibusuki City Council for the first photograph. The picture, taken in 1978, can be seen in Clarke's book, although it does not show very much. The object was in view for only a very short time. Also in 1978 a Mr M. Omagari took a picture of two Issies together, and later that year more than twenty people saw Issie in the middle of the lake. A local builder, Yutaka Kawaji, said, 'Two big humps each 5 m long and 0.5 m high were swimming for about two minutes. There was another 5 m between each hump and the skin was very dark.' He claimed to have seen the creature three times, the first when he was at primary school thirty years before. A monster (Kussie) is also reputed to inhabit L Kutcharo on the island of Hokkaido. It is alleged that there are photographs, a research programme and a K Protection Group, but credibility is undermined by the fact that in 1938 the lake was poisoned with acid after an earthquake.[254]

There are reports of lake creatures from many other countries, but details are scarce and probably unreliable. Nowhere is there anything like the amount of data available from L Ness.

8
Epilogue:
Summary and a Personal View

The evidence for the existence of N stands or falls on the modern evidence (since 1933); prehistoric myths offer no sort of evidence and nor does Adomnan. After cross-examination how has this evidence fared?

In chapter 2 I grouped the eyewitness reports according to the phenomenon which might explain them, and it is my view that they are all so explained. The most obvious are the wave-like reports. It seems that although modern reports of N may have been instigated by sight of an otter, the ubiquitous notion that N is huge, that it has many humps or coils, and that it creates a large surface disturbance comes from misperceptions of surface waves or wakes, particularly 'standing waves'. The naive belief of N-hunters that N appears in calm weather ('Nessie weather') is seen to be a misunderstanding of the fact that unusual wave phenomena are practically only seen on a flat calm surface.

There has always been more interest in reports of N on land, and several of them are classics. However, allowing for a certain amount of exaggeration, compounded by fright, the reports make sense as accounts of encounters with otters, even the MacKay report which started the modern legend. Dinsdale noted that on occasion white markings have been observed on the throat and cheeks of N,[255] but he did not point out (or did not know) that these markings are characteristic of the otter. The habit of the otter in rising and sinking vertically when making a long neck explains many reports of N performing this manoeuvre. Several observers appear to have caught an otter away from the water, causing it to make a sudden dash, even crossing a road. The picture drawn by the Spicers appears to show an otter which, having started to cross the road, turned when it heard the car. What is usually taken to be the head is actually the tail. Arthur Grant's inability to recognise an otter (despite his profession) may be explained by the darkness and the probability that he was no more familiar with otters than anyone else. Veterinary surgeons are rarely called to treat otters. The evidence seems to support the reasonable contention that the nearer the witnesses were, the more their description resembles that of an otter, with land observations being more accurate than those where the creature was in the water. The description given by the two girls (MacDonald/Harvey), who claimed to have been only 20 m away, is very close to that of an otter.

The belief that N not only has many humps or undulations but two horns appears to stem almost entirely from the Finlay report, which is clearly derived from misperception of a young roe deer.

Plainly eyewitness evidence for N is not to be relied on. All modern eyewitnesses have heard that N lives in L Ness, and whether or not they consciously admit it they are psychologically prepared to see N at some time or other. Even some who came with scepticism have departed as believers because they were not well enough informed about the tricks that L Ness can play.

Science is not satisfied with eyewitness evidence; it prefers evidence unprocessed by the human observer. It is not even satisfied with the unsupported claims of scientists. Science demands instrumental data, and preferably repeatable data. In the case of a rare phenomenon there can be no expectation of repeatability, but where a phenomenon like N is restricted to a particular domain there ought to be a high probability that it can be detected by extended observation.

Since one of the simplest and commonest data recorders is the camera, there ought to be many photographs of N. But the photographic evidence is poor. Of the twenty-one still photographs, it seems that seven (P1, P2, P6, P9, P15, P19, P21) are hoaxes, five (P7, P8, P10, P11, P13) are of natural phenomena, and six (P3, P4, P5, P14, P18, P20) provide insufficient data for evaluation. Of the fifteen pictures known to Mackal, he accepted only P1, P5, and P6 as positive evidence, but two of these are almost certainly hoaxes and so little is known about P5 that it cannot be regarded as evidence, and it has indications of a hoax. Of the remaining five pictures which provide insufficient data, it seems very likely that they are of natural phenomena, inanimate objects (natural or man-made), or hoaxes. In that case there is no acceptable still photograph of N.

Surprisingly there are more cine films that are alleged to show N than there are still photographs, but this may be due to the effort of the LNIB. Some show very little and some have never been seen. Mackal accepted only five (F3, F4, F6, F7, F15) as positive evidence, and he considered the remainder to be unacceptable as evidence.[256] In fact too little is known about either F3 or F4 to reach a conclusion, and F6 is now known to be of a dead horse. It seems that F15 shows a wake effect, and the only film left in Mackal's evidence is F7. However F7 is a film of a boat, a fact that ought to have been recognised long ago. Of more recent films, the only one with a substantial image is F26, which may show an inanimate object manipulated by two schoolboys. Among all the cine films there is not one which unequivocally shows anything that a scientist would accept as N; it appears that they all show common objects or phenomena (with the possibility that a few are hoaxes). Beckjord's video sequence surely shows the splash of water birds, as Hepple claimed, and Pollock's video might show anything.

Frustrated and disappointed by the failure of above-water photography, many had high hopes of underwater exploration and much has been made of the results obtained by the AAS. However, there is mystery regarding the provenance of U1/2 and suspicion that an artist has been at work on them. One is not reassured by Wyckoff's explanation, which is undermined by both the discoveries of Razdan and Kielar and my own experience. Of course Wyckoff could justify his claim by releasing unenhanced negatives to independent enhancement laboratories. Nevertheless there is a high probability that U1/2 show bottom debris, probably tree branches or roots, caught as the camera was carried by *Nan* towards the sloping bottom of Urquhart Bay.

A clear explanation has emerged for U4/5; the pictures which the AAS proudly claim show N's head, neck and upper torso are evidently pictures of the bed of L Ness (and objects lying on it), taken as the camera rig rolled and tumbled in the shallows.

None of the underwater pictures show any evidence for the existence of N, and it is relevant to point out that when the AAS attempted to take pictures in 1976 from a securely anchored rig they had no success.

As some have pointed out, photography is very limited underwater, especially in the gloom of L Ness, and it can monitor only a very small sample of a very large volume. It can be argued that the failure of underwater photography was only to be expected and that other methods ought to be employed. The one instrument that ought to detect N if it exists is sonar. Unfortunately sources of deception affecting sonar are as numerous if not more numerous than those affecting vision above water. Very few of the hunters who have used sonar have been skilled in its use, and none of the sonar apparatus was originally designed to hunt N.

It was natural that the curious crews of fishing boats would try out their echo-sounders in L Ness, and evidently some were misled by fish shoals. S1 is the only known sonar hoax, and most of the reports are probably genuine cases of mistaken identity. As the Loch Ness and Morar Project has shown, the more controls that are introduced the less spectacular and mysterious the targets become. This is a clear indication that with full and adequate controls there would be no mysterious targets.

What has become the classic sonar evidence for the existence of N (S11) is now shown to be the result of methodological errors and ignorance. The AAS's interpretation of the sonar chart is clearly untenable and a satisfactory alternative explanation exists. The Academy's so-called experts cannot have had any idea of the circumstances in which the recording was obtained, but even so their ability to interpret sonar charts must be questioned. All the estimates of the size of the 'large creatures' are unjustified and seem to be the result of wishful thinking and ignorance. There is absolutely no evidence that the chart shows creatures, parts of which were simultaneously photographed by the camera-strobe, and one suspects that there has been a tendency to interpret the sonar traces in terms of the pictures, and vice versa. Each has its own mundane explanation and neither offers any evidence for the existence of N. Examination of the results obtained by The Loch Ness and Morar Project indicates that their 1982 'targets' were side wall returns. In short, there is no sonar evidence for N.

Not only has the positive sonar evidence turned out to be negative, but there is a lack of the sort of evidence that ought to exist. Although hydrophones have occasionally detected some unidentified sounds, which may have had a mechanical origin, there has been no sign of the echo location signals that we would expect a blind underwater species to emit. Furthermore, a deliberate sonar search of the lake found nothing. Not enough attention has been drawn to the most important and definitive experiment ever conducted in L Ness. S5 was a sweep of the lake with sonar so that N either had to run before the sonic 'net' or be detected by it. It was therefore an acceptable test of both H_o and H_n, and its negative result must mean that H_n is false. It is special pleading to argue that the negative result was due to N hiding in caves or in the bottom mud; if N exists there must be many N and some would have been caught by the 'net' in mid-water. In 1962 Baker and Westwood showed that N does not exist. I predict that although some will continue to search, and although there will occasionally be what appears to be positive evidence, nothing will ever be found. The null hypothesis applies.

Not only does the evidence show that N does not exist, N's existence is not probable. H_n relies strongly on what Dinsdale calls 'a most important fact':[257] the belief that plesiosaur-type N entered L Ness from the sea at the end of the last ice-age. However, it has not yet been established that L Ness was ever open to the sea; a 4 m core, which probably sampled 11,000 years of sediment, showed no sign of marine creatures.[258] This result agrees with H_o, but it does not agree with H_n. Then the population of N has been estimated to be at least 10 (with upper limits ranging from 20 to 1000);[259] even a population of 10 N would make their presence felt in L Ness. However, such a population would not be viable due to inbreeding.[260] H_o explains why not one has been found. The temperature of L Ness (6 °C in the hypolimnion) is too cold for any of the ancient plesiosaurs, which became extinct 65 million years ago, and there is no reason to suppose that some could have adapted. No reptile is known to tolerate such cold conditions. Halstead *et al.*, apart from wondering how a former tropical marine reptile could endure the cold water of L Ness, and how it survived for 64 million years before it could enter the lake, pointed out that there were two major types of plesiosaur: the long-necked, which fed on fish in the surface waters, and the streamlined large-headed forms, which fed on cephalopods and could dive to depths of 300 m. While N appears to be a long-necked variety, its behaviour in diving is that of the other plesiosaur. They noted that it is 'inherently improbable' that there would emerge a mixture of the two groups.[261] In other words, N's appearance and behaviour do not agree with any known species of plesiosaur. If N entered L Ness from the sea, then its relatives ought to be roaming the seas yet, especially the tropical seas which were the original home of the species. But no plesiosaurs are extant anywhere in the world, a fact consistent with H_o.

The null hypothesis is supported in a curious way by Binns's observation that the more L Ness is watched the less N shows itself.[262] This is what would be expected if N does not exist. If reports are merely due to misinterpretations of the commonplace at distances too great to allow proper identification and/or by inexperienced observers, then saturating the surroundings with skilled observers is bound to reduce or even eliminate reports of N. The skilled observer sees what the unskilled sees, but knows that it is not N and so does not report it.

The conclusion I have reached justifies the view of E. G. Boulenger, Director of the Aquarium at London Zoo in 1933, who said in that year that the reports of N were 'a striking example of mass hallucination'. He noted how, once N was said to have been seen by a few people, it would be reported by many more.[263] Sir Arthur Keith thought that the very large number of people claiming to have seen N proved that it was imaginary and that they were seeing what they wanted to see.[264] Gould allowed the possibility that he had assisted various honest but self-deluded persons to create a zoological myth.[265] I am sure that this is what he did; Whyte, Holiday, Dinsdale, Witchell, and Mackal have all done the same.

The word 'monster' has several definitions, but one in particular is appropriate to this conclusion – 'an imaginary animal compounded of incongruous elements, e.g. centaur, sphinx, griffin'. The popular N is indeed an incongruous mix of reptile and mammal, of fish and amphibian, of vertebrate and invertebrate, of long-necked and short-necked plesiosaur, of seal, whale, eel, etc. It is a chimera, no more real than the centaur or the griffin.

I placed N as the archtype and sample of a set of lake-monsters and determined that the existence of all such creatures stands or falls with the fate of N. If N does not exist there are no monsters in any lake in the world. Not all the evidence from other lakes has been explained here, but most of it is similar to evidence for N. Consequently similar conclusions can be drawn. The Fletcher photograph of 'Ogopogo' is obviously a picture of a heavy ship wake, and the same is probably true of Folden's film. The Vincent/Konefall photograph probably shows a floating tree trunk.

In my view there is absolutely no reason why anyone should believe in the existence of lake-monsters.

Notes and References

*indicates that full details are in the Bibliography
pb = paperback edition

1   'Strange spectacle on Loch Ness', *Inverness Courier*, 2 May 1933.
2   Moon,* p. 28.
3   Costello (1975),* p. 169.
4   Grimshaw and Lester,* p. 4.
5   Grimshaw and Lester,* p. 5.
6   Mackal (1980),* pp. 210–11.
7   In fact these models were not shown at the Great Exhibition; they were constructed in Crystal Palace Park at Sydenham, where the Exhibition building was re-erected and re-opened in 1854.
8   Grimshaw and Lester,* pp. 8–11.
9   Bauer.*
10 British Museum (Natural History); *Scientific Research* (London, 1956); also reported in the *Sunday Post*, 27 July 1952.
11 John Murray and Laurence Pullar, *Bathymetrical Survey of the Freshwater Lochs of Scotland*, Vol. II (Edinburgh, 1910), pp. 428–9.
12 David Stirling of the Federation of British Columbian Naturalists, in Moon,* p. 135.
13 Peter Baker and Mark Westwood, 'Sounding out the monster', *The Observer*, 26 August 1962.
14 Letter to author, 22 August 1984.
15 Laurence Draper of the Institute of Oceanographic Sciences, in a letter to author, 7 November 1984.
16 Mackal (1976),* pp. 28–9.
17 Maurice Burton, in a letter to author, received 27 October 1984.
18 See my article 'The key to the loch?' in *British Journal of Photography* (Sep. 1988), pp. 12–13.
19 Peter F. Baker, 'Objects seen in Loch Ness', *The Scotsman*, 13 September 1960.
20 as note 19.
21 Dinsdale (1961),* p. 63.
22 Gould,* p. 107.
23 Campbell,* pp. 69–70.
24 Burton,* *passim*.
25 Binns,* Plates 6(a) and 6(b).

26   as note 19.
27   Maurice Burton, 'The World of Science – The Problem of the Loch
     Ness Monster: A Scientific Investigation (2)', *The Illustrated London
     News* (23 July 1960), pp. 150–2.
28   as note 13.
29   Gould,* pp. 110–12.
30   Burton,* pp. 132–5.
31   Letter of 22 December 1815 to Mr Morritt.
32   Costello (1975),* p. 149.
33   See C. J. Harris, *Otters – A Study of the Recent Lutrinae* (London 1968).
34   Mackal (1976),* p. 82.
35   Mackal (1980),* p. 205.
36   Mackal (1976),* p. 185.
37   Gould,* p. 94.
38   O. L. Zangwill, 'Abnormalities of memory', in *Encyclopaedia Britannica.*
39   Robert Buckhout, 'Eyewitness Testimony', *Scientific American*
     (December 1974), 231 (6), 23–31.
40   Mackal (1976),* p. 84.
41   *Adomnan's Life of Columba,* edited and translated, with notes, by Alan
     Orr Anderson and Marjorie Ogilvie Anderson (London, 1961), II, 27.
42   Grimshaw and Lester,* pp. 3–4.
43   Binns,* pp. 54–5
44   Costello (1975),* p. 167.
45   Witchell (1975[pb]),* p. 56.
46   *Inverness Courier,* 6 November 1962.
47   Witchell (1975[pb]) p. 29; Gould,* pp. 36–7.
48   Witchell (1975[pb]),* p. 79.
49   Welfare and Fairley,* p. 111.
50   'Nessie's "trial run" witnessed by holidaymakers', *The Press and Journal*
     (Aberdeen), 18 September 1979.
51   'Nessie's spectacular show', *The Press and Journal* (Aberdeen), 1
     September 1979.
52   Costello (1975),* p. 34.
53   Gould,* pp. 56–8.
54   *The Scotsman,* 23 October 1933; Gould,* pp. 70–1.
55   *The Scotsman,* 31 August 1938.
56   Dinsdale (1972),* p. 107.
56A 'Close encounter on Loch Ness', *The Press and Journal,* 24 June 1993 and
     'Nessie media mania!', *The Press and Journal,* 25 June 1993.
57   Hector F. Whitehead, in a letter to *The Scotsman,* 17 September 1960.
58   Gould,* p. 28.
59   Gould,* p. 29.
60   Costello (1975),* p. 31.
61   *Northern Chronicle,* 3 September 1930.
62   *Northern Chronicle,* 10 September 1930.
63   Clive Limpkin, 'The birth of the Loch Ness Monster', *Daily Mail*
     (London), 25 March 1983.
64   Gould,* pp. 39–40.
65   Costello (1975),* p. 81.
66   Costello (1975),* p. 75.
67   Witchell (1975[pb]),* p. 122.

68 Witchell (1975[pb]),* p. 123.
69 Witchell (1975[pb]),* p. 139.
70 Witchell (1975[pb]),* pp. 89–90.
71 Witchell (1975[pb]),* p. 90.
72 Witchell (1975[pb]),* pp. 91–2.
73 Witchell (1975[pb]),* pp. 92–4.
74 Costello (1975),* p. 36.
75 Binns,* p. 20.
76 Costello (1975),* p. 38
77 Costello (1975),* pp. 38–9.
78 Burton,* p. 152.
79 Witchell (1975[pb]),* p. 96.
80 Costello (1975),* p. 54.
81 Witchell (1975),* pp. 97–8.
82 Costello (1975),* p. 86.
83 Carruth,* p. 19.
84 Carruth,* p. 14.
85 Gould,* p. 13.
86 Whyte (1957),* p. 3.
87 Costello (1975),* p. 40.
88 Gould,* p. 23.
89 Dinsdale (1973),* p. 75.
90 Burton,* p. 78.
91 Binns,* p. 99.
92 Maurice Burton, 'Verdict on Nessie', *New Scientist* (23 January 1969), p. 191.
93 Mackal (1976),* p. 98.
94 David K. Caldwell and Melba C. Caldwell, 'Consider the Loch Ness Monster: Fact, Fiction or Pilot Whale?', *Underwater Nature* (1970), 6(3), 16–17.
95 Maurice Burton, 'The Loch Ness Saga', *New Scientist* (24 June, 1 and 8 July 1982).
96 Witchell (1975[pb]),* pp. 65–9.
97 For full analysis see my 'The Surgeon's Monster Hoax', *British Journal of Photography* (20 April 1984), pp. 402–5/410. See also Paul H. LeBlond and Michael Collins, 'The Wilson Nessie Photo: A Size Determination Based on Physical Principles', *Cryptozoology* 6 (1987), pp. 55–64 and my comments (and LeBlond's response) in *Cryptozoology* 8 (1989) pp. 129–135.
97A James Langton, 'Revealed: the Loch Ness picture hoax' and 'Nessie and a big-game hunter's monster ego', *The Sunday Telegraph*, 13 March 1994. See also Boyd and Martin's 'Creating a monster' in *BBC Wildlife*, April 1994.
97B *The Sunday Telegraph*, 20 March 1994 and *BBC Wildlife*, August 1994.
98 'The most astonishing Loch Ness story yet', *Scottish Sunday Express* (15 July 1951).
99 Brendan Kemmet, 'Is the monster picture a FAKE?', *Scottish Sunday Express* (22 July 1951).
100 Burton,* p. 74.
101 Mackal (1976),* p. 102.
102 Binns,* p. 100.

102A Witchell (1989pb),* p. 83.
103   Witchell (1975pb),* pp. 87–8.
104   MacNab's picture was not included in Whyte's book until the revised edition of 1961.
105   Mackal (1976),* p. 276.
106   as note 92.
107   Binns,* p. 102.
108   Witchell (1975pb),* pp. 86–7.
109   Mackal (1976),* p. 104.
110   W. H. Lehn, 'Atmospheric refraction and lake monsters', *Science* (13 July 1979), 205; 183–5.
111   Binns,* p. 102.
112   Mackal (1976),* p. 105.
113   Maurice Burton, in a letter to author, received 27 October 1984.
114   Mackal (1976),* p. 106.
115   Witchell (1975pb),* pp. 105–6; Mackal (1976),* pp. 107–8.
116   Mackal (1976),* p. 110.
117   See Mary Beith and Ian Sharp, 'I'm no fraud says Frank the Loch Ness Monster hunter', *Sunday Mail* (15 August 1976); Witchell (1975pb),* pp. 126–7; Mackal (1976),* p. 111; my 'The "Monster" Tree-trunk of Loch Ness', *The Skeptical Inquirer* (Winter 1982–83), 7 (2), 42–6; Binns,* pp. 104–6.
118   Stewart McCulloch, '14 hours with the monster – full story...', *Sunday Express* (5 October 1975); Alan Wilkins, 'Monster: The Four vital sightings', *The Field* (27 November 1975), pp. 1047–8; Alan Wilkins, 'The shapes on the loch', *The Field* (4 December 1975), p. 1096.
119   Bob Rickard, 'Nessie: The Shiels 1977 Photos', *Fortean Times* (Summer 1979), 29; 26–31.
120   Bob Rickard, 'GSW examines Doc's Nessie photos', *Fortean Times* (Winter 1978), 24; 14–16.
121   Tom Bearden, 'Nessie photos & the new physics', letter to *Fortean Times* (Spring 1978), 25; 49–50; in fact we inhabit a 4D universe!
122   Dinsdale (1982),* p. 187.
123   See my article 'The doctored Nessie Photographs' in *The Photographic Journal* 130/1 (January 1990), pp. 42–44
124   Rip Hepple, *Nessletter* 52 (June 1982); letter from Cato to author dated 13 November 1984.
125   John Gradon, 'We've seen Loch Ness Monster', *The Calgary Sunday Sun* (5 September 1982); Rip Hepple, *Nessletter* 54 (October 1982).
126   Charles Fraser, 'Definite proof that Nessie exists', *Evening Express* (Aberdeen) (18 September 1973).
127   Witchell (1975pb),* p. 38.
128   Mackal (1976),* p. 290.
129   Burton,* p. 78.
130   Witchell (1975pb),* pp. 52–3.
131   Burton,* pp. 72–3.
132   Costello (1975),* p. 77.
133   Costello (1975),* pp. 77–8.
134   Burton,* Figs. 18 and 19, pp. 67–71, 83–5.
135   Now the Southampton Oceanography Centre (University of Southampton).

136 Maurice Burton in letter to author dated 8 October 1984.
137 Mackal (1976),* pp. 117–18.
138 as note 126.
139 Dinsdale (1961),* pp. 77–91.
140 *Report on a film taken by Tim Dinsdale*, with an introduction by David James (n.d. but known to be 1966); see also an appendix in Costello,* and parts of two original pages in Dinsdale (1975),* p. 12. The leaflet and Costello's version contain transcription errors, although Costello has corrected some of those in the leaflet.
141 See my Article 'Monster or boat?', *The Photographic Journal* 126, 2 (February 1986), 54–8.
142 Mackal gives date as '18 October'.
143 Witchell (1975^{pb}),* p. 108.
144 Mackal (1976),* pp. 290–1.
145 Witchell (1975^{pb}),* pp. 100–1; Mackal (1976),* p. 291.
146 Witchell (1975^{pb}),* p. 110; Mackal (1976),* pp. 291–2. Mackal appears to have the wrong location.
147 Witchell (1975^{pb}),* p. 111; Mackal (1976),* p. 292.
148 James,* pp. 30–1.
149 Mackal (1976),* pp. 292–3.
150 Witchell (1975^{pb}),* p. 114; James,* pp. 31–3; Mackal (1976),* p. 121.
151 James,* pp. 32–4; Mackal (1976),* p. 292.
152 Dinsdale (1982),* pp. 188–98.
153 Not to be confused with the International Society of Cryptozoology.
154 Rip Hepple, *Nessletter* 59, 60, 61 (August–December 1983).
154A 'Lochside video footage shortens odds on Nessie', *Scotsman*, 12 March 2002.
155 Robert H. Rines (with Harold E. Edgerton, Charles W. Wyckoff and Martin Klein), 'Search for the Loch Ness Monster', *Technology Review* (March/April 1976), 78 (5), 25–40.
156 'A computer aids in search for "Nessie"', *Caltech News* (December 1975).
157 Some have claimed that the 'flipper' was at least 6 m from the camera with length estimates varying from 2 to 3 m (see LNIB Press Release dated 29 October 1972).
158 R. Demak, 'The (Retouched) Loch Ness Monster', Skeptical Eye column, *Discover* (September 1984), 5 (9), 6. See also Razdan and Kielar, 'Sonar and Photographic Searches for the Loch Ness Monster: a Reassessment'; *The Skeptical Inquirer* (Winter 1984–85), 9 (2), 147–58.
159 Charles W. Wyckoff, unpublished letter to *Discover* dated 27 August 1984 (copy provided by Henry H. Bauer). Letter since published in *Nessletter* 67 (December 1984).
160 L. B. Halstead (with P. D. Goriup and J. A. Middleton), letter to *Nature* (15 January 1976), 259; 75–6.
161 Sir Peter Scott, letter to *Nature* (15 January 1976) 259:76.
162 Mackal (1976),* p. 277.
163 *Daily Record* (Glasgow) (25 November 1975).
164 His calculation, that D_n = 84 cm is based on a minimum circle of confusion of 1/30th mm and ignores refraction.
165 With camera angles (allowing for refraction) of 33° x 43° the picture plane at 1.5 m is 88 x 117 cm. Since object is about ⅕ of frame width and ⅓ of frame height it must be 29 cm high by 23.5 cm wide.

166   G. E. Harwood, 'Interpretation of the 1975 Loch Ness Pictures',
       Progress in Underwater Science (1977), 2: 83–90 (discussion pp. 99–102).
167   Richard H. Raynor, letter to author in early September 1984.
168   Some claim that it shows an engine block used as a mooring weight.
169   Adrian Shine, 'Sounding out the sightings', *The Unexplained* (1980), 1
       (12), 226–9.
170   Peter F. Baker and Mark Westwood, 'Under-water detective work', *The
       Scotsman* (14 September 1960).
171   D. J. Creasey, 'On the use of sonar in Loch Ness searches', *Progress in
       Underwater Science* (1977), 2: 91–8 (discussion pp. 100–2).
172   as note 171.
173   Mackal (1976),* pp. 296–7; Creasey (as note 171); Dinsdale (1982),*
       Tables 1, 2 and 3.
174   *Daily Herald* (London) (6 December 1954).
175   as note 174.
176   *Daily Herald* (London) (7 December 1954).
177   *Daily Herald* (London) (18 December 1954).
178   Whyte (1957),* p. 16.
179   Witchell (1975pb),* pp. 85–6.
180   *The Scotsman* (5 December 1959).
181   Peter F. Baker and Richard Arnold, 'The Mystery of Loch Ness', *The
       Scotsman* (12 September 1960).
182   as note 170.
183   as note 13.
184   Later Professor P. F. Baker FRS, of King's College London (d. 1986).
185   Holiday,* p. 201.
186   D. Gordon Tucker and Hugh Braithwaite, 'Sonar picks up stirrings
       in Loch Ness', *New Scientist* (19 December 1969), pp. 664–6. See also
       University of Birmingham, Research and Publications (1968–69), 40: 49,
       and D. G. Tucker and D. J. Creasey, 'Some sonar observations in Loch
       Ness', *Proceedings of the Challenger Society* (1970), 4: 9–2.
187   Creasey later stated that the existence of this rock outcrop had been
       confirmed and that it *was* the cause of the reflection (as note 171, p.
       100).
188   'News and Views – Monsters by Sonar', *Nature* (28 December 1968),
       220: 1272.
189   As note 171, p. 97.
190   Mackal (1976),* pp. 31, 42, 298–302.
191   All data and quotation from Mackal (1976),* pp. 49, 305–6.
192   D. James *et al.*, *Annual Report of the Loch Ness Investigation Bureau* (1969),
       pp. 10–16; Mackal (1976),* pp. 303–5.
193   Mackal (1976),* p. 305.
194   Klein *et al.* (1972).*
195   The AAS had not claimed to have found caves.
196   Mackal (1976),* pp. 306–7.
197   No details of these have been published.
198   as note 155.
199   Meredith,* pp. 132–3.
200   Witchell (1975pb),* 130–1.
201   Now (Mrs) Hilary Green.
202   In the possession of Dick Raynor

203 Martin Klein and Charles Finkelstein, 'Sonar serendipity in Loch Ness', *Technology Review* (December 1976), 79 (2), 44–57. See also Edgerton/ Wyckoff, 'Loch Ness revisited', *IEEE spectrum*, February 1978, pp. 26–9.

204 Anthony Pledger, 'Sonar "sights" Nessie', *The Scotsman* (1 September 1978).

205 'They're sure it was Nessie', *The Sunday Post* (12 April 1981).

206 Adrian Shine, 'The biology of Loch Ness', *New Scientist* (17 February 1983), pp. 462–7; *Loch Ness Project Report* (1983); Tony Harmsworth, 'Assessment of the Project's Motives and Attitudes' (duplicated notes 24 July 1984).

207 Mackal (1976),* p. 297.

208 Mackal (1976),* p.308.

209 Hepple, *Nessletter* 59 (August 1983). See also Razdan and Kielar (as note 158).

210 Witchell (1975pb),* p. 107.

211 Hepple, *Nessletter* 47 (August 1981).

212 Dinsdale (1961),* p. 140.

213 Mackal (1976),* pp. 61–4, 78–9.

214 Mackal (1976),* p. 351.

215 ' "Monster" tracked by Radar', *The Scotsman* (22 August 1966).

216 Witchell (1975pb),* p. 122.

217 Bord,* Appendix 2.

218 Costello (1975),* p. 150.

219 Campbell,* pp. 138–40.

220 Mackal (1976),* pp. 50–1.

221 Hepple, *Nessletter* 51 (April 1982).

222 Loch Morar Survey, *Information Sheet* (January 1973).

223 Dinsdale (1976),* pp. 162–3.

224 as note 219, p. 152.

225 Costello (1975),* p. 194; Mackal (1976),* pp. 39–41.

226 Costello (1975),* pp. 209–11.

227 Costello (1975),* chap. 8.

228 Whyte (1957),* pp. 147–8.

229 Costello (1975),* p. 208.

230 Welfare and Fairley,* pp. 102–3.

231 Mackal (1980),* pp. 241–4.

232 Welfare and Fairley,* p. 105.

233 Mackal (1980),* pp. 244–5.

234 Welfare and Fairley,* p. 103.

235 Costello (1975),* p. 244.

236 Moon,* p. 52

237 Moon,* pp. 84–8.

238 Welfare and Fairley,* p. 104.

239 Moon,* pp. 94–6.

240 Welfare and Fairley,* pp. 103–5.

241 Moon,* p. 14.

242 Mackal (1980),* pp. 222–36.

243 Welfare and Fairley,* pp. 105–6.

244 Mackal (1980),* pp. 237–40.

245 Costello (1975),* p. 253.

246 W. H. Lehn and I. Schroeder, 'The Norse merman as an optical phenomenon', *Nature* (29 January 1981), 289: 363–6.
247 Mackal (1980),* p. 197; Costello (1975),* p. 239.
248 Mackal (1980),* pp. 217–18.
249 Zarzynski (1984),* *passim.*
250 Church, in *Pursuit* (1975), 8: 89–92.
251 Mackal (1980),* pp. 208–9.
252 Mackal (1980),* pp. 209–10.
253 Mackal (1980),* pp. 220–1.
254 Welfare and Fairley,* pp. 107–8.
255 Dinsdale (1961),* p. 13.
256 His summary on p. 294 is incorrect.
257 Dinsdale (1961),* p. 52.
258 Adrian Shine, *Loch Ness Project Report*, p. 11.
259 Carl Sagan, 'If there are any, could there be many', *Nature*, vol. 264, 9 Dec. 1976, p. 497. See also R. W. Sheldon and S. R. Kerr, 'The Population Density of Monsters in Loch Ness', *Limnology and Oceanography* (1972), vol. 17, pp. 796–8.
260 Richard Frankham and Katherine Ralls, 'Inbreeding leads to extinction', *Nature*, vol. 392, 2 Apr. 1998, pp. 441–2.
261 as note 160.
262 Binns,* p. 131.
263 *The Observer* (29 October 1933).
264 Costello (1975),* p. 55.
265 Gould,* p. 150.
266 David Martin and Alastair Boyd.*

Bibliography

pb indicates a paperback, and the superior numbers indicate edition

Books containing sections on lake-monsters

Bord, Janet and Colin, *Alien Animals* (London, 1980).
Cohen, Daniel, *A Modern Look at Monsters* (New York, 1970).
Dinsdale, Tim, *The Leviathans* (London, 1966, pb1976); as *Monster Hunt* (Washington, 1972).
Eberhart, George M., *Monsters: a Guide to Information on Unaccounted for Creatures* (New York, 1983), [bibliography].
Landsburg, Alan, *In Search of Myths and Monsters* (London, pb1977).
Mackal, Roy P., *Searching for Hidden Animals* (London, 1980).
Welfare, Simon and John Fairley (with introduction and comments by Arthur C. Clarke), *Arthur C. Clarke's Mysterious World* (London, 1980).

Books dealing with lake-monsters in general

Costello, Peter, *In Search of Lake Monsters* (London 1974; St Albans pb1975).

Books etc. dealing solely or mainly with the Loch Ness Monster

Akins, William, *The Loch Ness Monster* (New York, pb1977).
Bauer, Henry H., *The Enigma of Loch Ness: Making Sense of a Mystery* (Urbana and Chicago, 1986, pb1988, Stirling pb1991).
Baumann, Elwood David, *The Loch Ness Monster* (London, 1972).
Binns, Ronald (with R. J. Bell), *The Loch Ness Mystery Solved* (Shepton Mallet, 1983; London, pb1984; Buffalo, 1985).
Boyd, Alastair (see Martin).
Burton, Maurice, *The Elusive Monster* (London, 1961).
Carruth, J. A., *Loch Ness and its Monster* (Fort Augustus, ¹1938, ⁹1971), 24pp.
Dinsdale, Tim, *Loch Ness Monster* (London, ¹1961, ²1972, ³1976, ⁴1982, Philadelphia ¹1962, with added foreword).

—— *The Story of the Loch Ness Monster* (London, ᵖᵇ1973).

—— *Project Water Horse* (London, 1975).

—— *The Facts About Loch Ness and the Monster* (London, 1977) [wallchart].

Gould, Rupert, T., *The Loch Ness Monster and others* (London, 1934; reprinted New York, 1969, with added foreword).

Grimshaw, Roger, and Paul Lester, *The Meaning of the Loch Ness Monster* (Centre for Contemporary Cultural Studies, University of Birmingham, 1976, mimeograph), 42 pp.

Harmsworth, Anthony G., *The Mysterious Monsters of Loch Ness* (Huntingdon, 1980), 32 pp.

—— *Loch Ness: The Monster* (Tillicoultry, 1985), 32 pp.

Hastain, Ronald (ed., with Nicholas Witchell), *Loch Ness and its Monster* (Inverness, 1971), 48 pp.

Holiday, F. W., *The Great Orm of Loch Ness* (London, 1968, ᵖᵇ1971), with appendices by E. S. Richardson Jr and Peter Baker.

James, David, *Loch Ness Investigation* (London, undated), 40 pp.

Klein, Martin (with R. H. Rines, T. Dinsdale, and L. S. Foster), *Underwater Search at Loch Ness* (Concord, 1972).

Lane, W. H., *The Home of the Loch Ness Monster* (Edinburgh, 1934).

Mackal, Roy P., *The Monsters of Loch Ness* (London, 1976).

Macrae, Jim M., *Loch Ness Monster – Handbook* (Inverness, 1974), 15 pp.

Martin, David and Alastair Boyd, *NESSIE The Surgeon's Photograph Exposed* (East Barnet, 1999).

Meredith, Dennis L., *Search at Loch Ness* (New York, 1977).

Oudemans, A. C., *The Loch Ness Animal* (Leyden, 1934), 14 pp.

Owen, William, *Loch Ness revealing its Monsters* (Norwich, undated), 32 pp.

Robertson, Barrie, *Loch Ness and the Great Glen* (undated), 23 pp.

Searle, Frank, *Nessie: Seven Years in Search of the Monster* (Aylesbury, ᵖᵇ1976).

Whyte, Constance E., *The Loch Ness Monster* (Inverness, 1951), 13 pp.

—— *More Than a Legend* (London, ¹1957 , ²1961).

Witchell, Nicholas, *The Loch Ness Story* (Lavenham, ¹1974, ²1976; Harmondsworth, ᵖᵇ1975; London, ᵖᵇ1982, ᵖᵇ1989).

—— *Loch Ness and the Monster* (Newport, ¹1975, ²1976), 32 pp.

Books on other lake-monsters

Campbell, Elizabeth Montgomery (with David Solomon), *The Search for Morag* (London, 1972).

Moon, Mary, *Ogopogo: The Okanagan Mystery* (Vancouver, 1977).

Zarzynski, Joseph W., *Champ – Beyond the Legend* (New York, 1984).

Index